IN THE MOMENT

Real Life Stories of Hope and Inspiration

Compiled by Gary Doi

PREAMBLE

"Trial Island is a rocky picturesque piece of land with the commanding lighthouse near Oak Bay, BC. When I was living in Victoria during the 1960s I often visited that area for the solitude it provided from the big city. The sea, the running tide and the scent of the ocean reminded me of Kitkatla, my home village on the Northwest coast. I remember a time when I was fishing in the bay as a small pod of orcas approached nearby. Even though I had had many encounters with killer whales before, I was awe struck by the experience. I watched in wonderment as the majestic animals dove and returned to the surface in synchronized ballet-like movements. Years later, I tried to capture that moment in a painting called Trial Island."

– Roy Henry Vickers ("In the Moment" book cover)

Life is full of big, life-altering moments: graduating from school, finding your career path, falling in love, getting married, celebrating the birth of a child, suffering a loss, ending a marriage, retiring from work... The list goes on. Big moments are memorable, dramatic and public. They happen to all of us, in varying degrees. For better. For worse.

Then there are the small moments, like Roy's encounter with killer whales. Not newsworthy perhaps, but noteworthy nonetheless. These moments catch you by surprise, injecting wonder and awe into your day. They challenge you to become more open, mindful and curious. That is especially important when life is fractured and fast-paced as it often is in our 'Age of Distraction'.

The collection of short stories in this anthology is about the moments in life – big and small. It's organized into three interrelated sections: Moments in Time, Moments of Insight and Moments that Matter. Of course, they are not mutually exclusive; they mix together and blend just like life itself. For example, Gold medal-list and BC Hall of Famer Ivan McLelland (Penticton, BC) writes about that moment as a 26-year-old when he was offered a professional hockey contract with the Montreal Canadiens. Outdoor enthusiast Derm Kennedy (Kimberley, BC) describes the experience of helping his young friend with cerebral palsy climb to the peak of Mount Fisher. Entrepreneur Deborah Fike (Eugene, Oregon) describes her father-in-law's joyous outlook on life and the legacy he left behind. Native Elder Roberta Price (Richmond, BC) speaks openly and honestly about her healing journey after years of abuse, discrimination and suffering while in the foster care system. Whitey Bernard (Tofino, BC) featured in the famous World War 2 photograph "Wait for me, Daddy", shares his fascinating story about the human cost of war on his family.

As with all the books in the Inspiring Hope Series, prominent Canadian artist Roy Henry Vickers generously provided the glorious artwork for the book cover and section dividers. Roy also crafted a beautiful story titled 'Rainbow Alley', in which he recalls his early days growing up in a small, native coastal village.

Profits from this book benefit the Children's Wish Foundation. Children's Wish is a uniquely Canadian charity that helps Canadian children, families and communities by granting the favourite wish of a child diagnosed with a life-threatening illness. Every wish granted creates moments of joy that ease the pain of a child, give respite to the child's family and connect healthcare professionals and communities. We've featured some of their stories in the opening section of the book.

I owe a debt of gratitude to Zee Gorman from San Francisco, California. She, once again, seamlessly managed the online publishing process and created the beautiful design work for this book. Her creativity, passion and artistic talent are evident throughout.

I am also indebted to writer Marion Iberg for the valuable feedback she provided. Marion always seems to know what works as a coherent story and whether the writer achieved what he/she was striving for.

An added feature of this particular book is the special section called "Community Partners". Various businesses and organizations signed on as Community Partners and generously purchased books in advance of its release. In exchange, we were happy to provide display ad space to acknowledge their support. Special thanks to friends – Ivan McLelland and Bob Cade – for working tirelessly to ensure that Community Partners became an integral part of the book.

To all of the writers represented in this anthology, I would like to extend my heartfelt appreciation. I am grateful to them for their openness and courage in sharing their personal stories of hope and inspiration. It has been a privilege to work with such talented and committed individuals.

And, finally, my deepest thanks to you (the readers) for taking the stories to heart and sharing them with others.

Enjoy the moment.

Gary Doi, Creator of the
Inspiring Hope Book Series,
September 2016

ISBN-13: 978-1535453882
ISBN-10: 1535453885

To All Those Who Inspire Hope

CONTENTS

Inspiring Hope Book Series

Available on Amazon.com/ca/uk

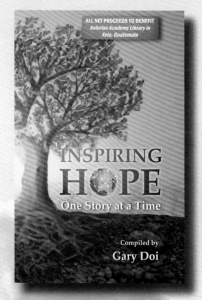

One Story at a Time, 2013

Fly Like an Eagle, 2014

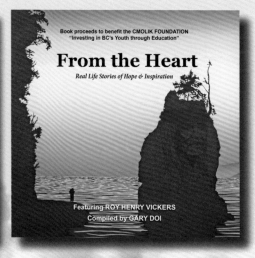

From the Heart, 2015

Moments That Matter

Community Partners

(Ogden Point Breakwater, Victoria, BC; Photo credit: Gary Doi)

Thank you for picking up this anthology, *In the Moment*. The proceeds of this book benefit The Children's Wish Foundation of Canada, and help us fulfill the wishes of some very deserving children who are facing life-threatening illnesses.

As a mother, I am consistently inspired by the work we do at Children's Wish. Seeing the impact a wish can have on a sick child reminds me every day to be grateful for the small things, the small moments that make life worthwhile.

Simple things like a trip to spend some quality time with family, or receiving a gift when you're having a hard time. These things can become the stuff of wishes for our children and their families when their life unexpectedly becomes taken over by endless doctor's visits and treatment plans.

After meeting families like the two whose stories you will read in this book - families who face such overwhelming medical challenges - I am always glad to know there is something I can do to bring joy and wonder to young lives that are fraught with uncertainty. By purchasing this book and supporting Children's Wish, you are now a part of creating that joy.

To learn more about how you can refer an eligible child for their wish, or to donate, visit www.childrenswish.ca

Thank you.

Jennifer Petersen
Director – BC & Yukon Chapter
The Children's Wish Foundation of Canada

Marko's Story

By Bianca Marconato (Coquitlam, BC)

My brother Marko was born on November 8th, 1999. Mom told me he was a healthy baby, and a happy one. At the age of three, Marko wanted to play hockey and after falling in love with the game, he dreamt of being a goalie in the NHL.

Marko's world changed on January 25th, 2012 when he was diagnosed with bone cancer, Osteosarcoma. From that day forward Marko would spend two years at BC Children's Hospital undergoing chemotherapy and receiving treatment for other illnesses caused by the aggressive treatment to cure his cancer. At the time, Marko was only in grade six and it was hard for him to focus on his treatment and let everything else go – his hockey, his family, and his friends. However, Marko was brave and still sported a proud smile on his face throughout his entire treatment.

On April 24th, 2012 Marko would undergo his first surgery, but it wouldn't be the last. The doctors were thinking about removing his arm, but after some careful planning they realized they could possibly try and save it. The doctors predicted the surgery would be around 10-12 hours. In reality, it ended up taking 20 hours. The procedure was to remove the fibula from his right leg and put it in his arm to replace the cancerous bone. The surgery was a success and doctors executed their plan precisely. When Marko awoke he still had his right arm and knew he could one day block pucks in his net again.

Marko thankfully was able to fight his cancer and gained remission status in September of 2012, but his journey would not end there.

He would spend the next year in and out of Children's Hospital with various infections and major organ problems, all caused by the aggressive cancer treatment. Marko continued to miss out on sports, school, and time with his friends; it was devastating for him and his family.

In 2014, Marko was declared cancer free and hoping to get back to his old life, but it wasn't easy to pick up where he had left off when he was first diagnosed. Marko is now 16 years old and trying to figure out life. He has been back on the ice, but still deals with some health issues, taking things one step at a time and living life to the fullest. As a grade 11 student at Terry Fox Secondary School, Marko still plays hockey with a passion – he will always play the sport.

Marko is a very loving brother and friend who is always happy and wears a proud smile on his face daily. He will always be my hero after being alongside him while in a war for his life. He fought long and hard and continues to teach me that I can do or be anything I desire. Marko is determined to do and try anything he can despite his physical limitation.

In February 2016, Marko and our family went on the trip of a lifetime with The Children's Wish Foundation, visiting Universal Studios in Orlando, followed by a Caribbean Cruise. It was a wonderful opportunity to relax and spend time together and celebrate all we have overcome as a family.

(Marconato Family at Jurassic Park: Bianca, Nicco, Dad, Wish Kid Marko & Mom)

Bianca Marconato is 14 years old, and the sister of 16 year old cancer survivor Marko. She is an avid athlete who enjoys competitive swimming, water polo and volleyball. Bianca hopes to attend university and become a Pediatric Oncologist after graduating from high school.

In the Moment — Real Life Stories of Hope and Inspiration

People are like birds.

There are peacocks who love to strut their stuff and show off what they've got. There are ostriches who stick their heads in the sand and refuse to deal with reality. You have vultures who prey on you when you're down. There are dodo birds. Everyone knows a dodo bird. They are like chickens – they can't fly.

But there is one bird that is different and distinct from all the rest. It is the eagle. The eagle is a special bird. The eagle is a solitary creature that soars high above the rest; but its true defining characteristic is its eyesight. Its vision.

Faith's Disorder

By Natasha Prokosh (Coquitlam, BC)

(Natasha with a photo of her daughter Faith and her 3 children Lex, Gabe and JJ; Copyright 2016, Martinszabo.com)

This was the only explanation I could offer my 5-year-old son Gabe when he asked, "Why are my sisters different?" I had no answer for him. To be honest, I had the same question. Why did this happen to me? Why my girls? Doctors had no explanation.

I remember sitting with Gabe and telling him that sometimes life doesn't give us answers. Sometimes things happen that are out of our control and all we get to do is choose how we react to it. Choose how we see it. Choose whether we behave like an eagle or like a chicken. This is the analogy we would go back to continuously over the years. Years spent in and out of the hospital and doctors' offices. Years spent just trying to make it through the day. In the toughest and hardest days of my life I had to go back to that basic question: How am I going to see this?

Am I going to be the chicken or the eagle?

We became a team. A real family. We had seven years together, all of us. Faith, Alexa, and their two brothers, Gabe & JJ. And then Faith became ill.

Faith was more physically affected with this undiagnosed genetic disorder. Her health was much more fragile than Alexa's. Faith and I spent a lot of time in hospitals together. A lot. At the end of August 2013, just a few weeks after her 7th birthday, her liver failed. The doctors told me she was not expected to make it to the morning. But she did. She pulled through. She managed to stay strong for just over a week after that. She was transferred to Children's Hospital where doctors there had more experience dealing with situations like this.

My mother visited Faith and returned home to tell me Faith's breathing was becoming increasingly laboured and her vitals were dropping. Yet when the doctors would tell her to hang on and wait until mommy arrived, they would see her vitals and oxygen stats jump back up. They could actually see her fighting to stay alive until we said goodbye to each other.

I made it to her bedside with less than an hour before she would leave me. I was given the blessing of being able to tell her all the things I wanted to say before she died. I told her I loved her and that she was a gift in my life. I told her not to be scared and that we would see each other again. The last thing I told her was that I wouldn't forget her, and what I meant by that was I wouldn't let her be forgotten.

Medical Genetics at Children's Hospital approached my family about studying our DNA and finding the cause of why Alexa and Faith are the way they are. I didn't believe anything would come of it. It didn't matter to me either way. My girls were who they were and I loved them regardless. Dr. Boerkoel, a geneticist at Children's Hospital, would discover the mutation in the gene causing the disorder in my girls. He told me that the disease did not really have a name. It was called UNC80 because it was first identified in insects and worms. UNC stands for the word 'uncoordinated' and 80 is the gene number.

The name sucks. That's exactly what I told Dr. Boerkoel.

I also mentioned that to my friend Andy who works at Children's Wish. That's when he gave me a brilliant piece of advice.

"Tash, you should just rename it," said Andy. "Call it 'Faith's Disorder'. Start calling it that until it sticks, until everyone starts calling it that."

So that's what I did. I officially renamed this disorder – Faith's Disorder. I believe she has contributed much to the medical field and has earned the right to have this disorder named after her.

Natasha Prokosh and her 3 children Alexa, Gabe and JJ live in Coquitlam, BC. Her life's ambition is to teach her little eaglets to soar, which she does with the help of her mom, one of the greatest eagles she's ever met. Alexa has been approved for her wish and the family is looking forward to travelling somewhere warm where they can swim together!

Moments in Time

"In the end, it's not going to matter how many breaths you took, but how many moments took your breath away." - Shing Xiong

"Balance"— Roy Henry Vickers

MANO

By Derm Kennedy (Kimberley, BC)

(Manuel Miguel)

I first noticed Manuel Miguel in the preschool where my wife worked. Manuel (or Mano as he was called back then) had Cerebral Palsy, a neurological disorder that permanently affected his body movement and muscle coordination. Although he had normal intellectual function, his posture wasn't normal so, as a child, he had to wear metal braces on his skinny legs.

I came to know Mano several years later in about 1984, when he joined the Wolf Creek Cub Pack in the small rural community of Wasa, British Columbia. As is the tradition of the Cub Scout program, I was called "Akela", the leader of the pack. (Akela being the name of the lone wolf featured in Rudyard Kipling's Jungle Book.) The Cub Pack met weekly at the Wasa Elementary School gym and, on occasion, at Camp Stone near Kimberley and Blue Lake Camp, west of Canal Flats. Mano participated fully and most of the boys were happy to have him on their team despite his disability because he was funny, good natured and he never gave up. Mano always worked hard to complete tasks and his determination inspired the other boys.

But Mano did struggle.

One year, he tried to achieve his Skater's Badge. He practiced for weeks and weeks at the outdoor rink but his legs wobbled and buckled at the wrong times. His skating improved marginally but he still couldn't manage the required skills: he couldn't skate on one skate, go backwards or jump into the air and recover again. I tested him three times and each time I had to fail him.

"Sorry Mano," I said. "You've improved a lot. I'd like to give you the badge for how hard you worked but I'm not allowed to do that."

Mano didn't say anything. I knew he was disappointed.

"Mano, just think of the badges you have and the other kids don't," I said. "You have two interpreter's badges, one in French and one in Spanish."

"That's okay, Akela," he replied and walked away.

Learning to ride a bicycle was also a big challenge. Like most youngsters Mano started on a small two wheeler with training wheels. He probably crashed hundreds of times, mostly upon his launches and again when he wanted to dismount. His bike helmet protected his head but he still endured many scrapes and scratches from his falls. After months of "practice", the crashes were less frequent and his rides longer and faster. Soon he was enjoying the freedom of travelling the roads around Wasa Lake with friends, and biking to school, to Cubs and anywhere else he needed to be.

(Backside of Fisher Peak in the Summer – Photo Credit, Gary Doi)

After Grade 5, the children at our small neighbourhood school were bussed twenty-one miles to a much larger school in Kimberley, which enrolled Grades 6, 7 and 8 students. With that came many new experiences and challenges for Mano, not all of them good. He carried a small portable typewriter from class to class to take notes as his handwriting was slow and not legible. He was bullied because he looked different and had mobility issues. His Wasa friends stuck up for him but he was tormented by other students, which made school life difficult.

As Mano progressed through school he grew taller and his strength, particularly in his upper body and legs, continued to develop. When he was in Grade 10, I asked him to be my Cub Scout Pack Assistant which he readily accepted. Mano enjoyed working with the young boys and helping them with the projects and games. He was responsible, conscientious and a wonderful role model.

When his Grade 12 graduation year approached in 1992 I thought long and hard about a gift he'd appreciate, something he'd remember for a long time. Mano had developed into a kind, caring and determined young man who was an inspiration to others. I wanted a gift that would match his big-heartedness and drive to succeed.

"Mano, I'd like to talk to you about your grad gift," I began. "I've been thinking you might like to climb the summit of Mt. Fisher with me. Have you been up there yet?" I couldn't help myself. Of course, he hadn't been up there.

Mt. Fisher is the highest and most prominent peak of the southern Rocky Mountains in Canada. It is a popular climb, almost a rite of passage for adventuresome graduating students in the region. It is 9,300 feet above sea level and the hike is a 4,500 feet vertical accent from the parking area.

(Mt. Fisher in the early Spring – Photo Credit, Lyle Grisedale)

The hike normally takes 4 ½ hours up and 3 hours down. Mt. Fisher is not considered a technical climb, meaning no ropes, pitons and carabiners, but it's steep and long and there is some serious exposure near the top. I have taken people to the summit of Mt. Fisher many times but not someone with Cerebral Palsy. I didn't even know if it was possible. The whole idea was intriguing, but daunting.

"Well, would that interest you?" I asked.

"Really, Derm?" Mano replied. His eyes opened wide when he realized I wasn't kidding. "You'd take me up there? How would we do it?"

"We'd do it together, Mano," I said. "We'll find a way. We'll go sometime in July after your graduation. Okay?"

It was 5:00 am when my son Tim and I stopped by Mano's house. We wanted an early start on the hike as the afternoon summer temperatures could be intense.

"Well, are you ready for this, Mano?" I asked.

"I am, Derm," he said. "I've been looking at Mt. Fisher for weeks since you mentioned it. I can't believe I'm going to climb it."

It was still dark when we arrived at the trailhead parking lot. The beginning portion of the trail rose steeply through the timber. I was impressed with how Mano leaned into the slope and skillfully pulled on the low bushes for support. The first stretch of the hike was difficult, a good test for Mano and he didn't show any ill effects. We broke through the thick forest and reached the "first basin" in about an hour and a half. We stopped for a drink from the ice-cold mountain stream.

"Derm, this is awesome," he said. "The sun is shining through the trees. It's like a whole new world. Wow, I can't believe I'm here." The words came out quickly.

Effortlessly.

"We'll have even better views up there," I said, pointing to the next basin.

I picked up my backpack loaded with rope, clothes, food, water, climbing axe and safety gear and started up the hillside. The incline wasn't as steep as before but the path was rocky and not well defined. Hiking under those conditions had to be awkward for someone with Mano's mobility but he persevered and we managed to reach the "second basin" in decent time.

From there we could make out the trail ahead to where it petered out in a steep scree gully with vertical spires of towering black rock. I fastened a full-body harness on Mano and attached a short rope. I needed to support his balance on the steep, stone covered slope and keep him from falling backwards. Tim, who was about fourteen years old at the time, had climbed Fisher Peak before so he scrambled on ahead of us.

At the back of the bowl we hugged the mountain with our bodies as we climbed up the sliding scree. I held tightly to the rope as Mano tried to keep pace using his hands as anchors and shaky legs for traction. It was tough going and took twice the normal time. After reaching the narrow ridge—the saddle—we were ready for a well-deserved rest and a chance to take in the spectacular views.

"Wow!" said Mano to no one in particular. "I can see for miles and miles."

"Mt. Fisher is part of the Hughes Range of the Rocky Mountain Chain," I added. "To the west is the Kootenay River Valley which divides the Rockies from the Purcell Mountains.

"Cool."

"I'm proud of you Mano for making it this far," I said. "Now, we have a decision to make. At this point we are more than 4 ½ hours from the trail head and at least a hard hour to the summit. Many people don't

(Derm Kennedy)

In the Moment — Real Life Stories of Hope and Inspiration

make it this far. We're all pretty tired so it may wise to turn back here."

"Derm…" Mano took in a deep shaky breath. "Derm, I really want to make it to the top. Okay?"

"Okay, Mano, then that's what we'll do."

After our break we started up again; the summit was about 900 feet north of the saddle. Tim led the way along the narrow ridge. He knew to follow the yellow markers on the side of the rocks that mark the best route to the peak. With Mano firmly attached to me by rope, I led the way as we walked step by step up the narrow rocky path. It was slow going but we made steady progress.

The last 200 feet was the most technical. I tightened the tension on the rope as one slip would spell disaster. I was impressed with how Mano used his upper body to manoeuver over and around the slabs of rock. Things were going well until we came to the "crux"—a short rock wall that required pulling yourself up and over using your hands and feet. Mano tried several moves but struggled. At that point I felt there was no choice but to use the rope. So I braced myself on the ledge above him and hauled his 150 pound frame up and over that rock face. He scraped his bare legs in the process but he didn't complain one bit. After all, we had just made it to the top.

It was a glorious moment filled with emotion. We didn't have a camera to record the occasion but the image is branded in my memory. Here we were….Tim, Mano and I huddled shoulder to shoulder on that small, precipitous platform atop the tallest peak in the Southern Canadian Rockies.

"Wow, this is something!" said Mano, his eyes welling up with tears. "I can't believe we made it. Thanks Akela."

I held my breath for a second to keep from tearing up. I managed a weak smile and said, "Thanks, Mano. You made it. You did it. Congratulations buddy."

No one spoke for a long while. We knew the climb down could be tricky and would need to leave soon. Still, we probably sat there for ten or fifteen minutes—in silence. Taking in the stunning vistas. Thinking of the scope of our achievement. Feeling the happiness in our hearts.

Manuel Miguel graduated from Selkirk Secondary School in June 1992 and travelled ex-tensively throughout France the following year. Manuel earned his Bachelor of Arts Degree (1998) and Bachelor of Education Degree (2000) from the University of Victoria in British Columbia. While attending university, Manuel commuted to school on his bicycle and, to this day, continues to bike to work daily when weather permits. He works full-time as a Teach-er-on-Call at several schools in the Victoria area as he enjoys the variety and flexibility his teaching career provides. Manuel's tenacity, humor and quiet determination has been an inspiration to his students, colleagues, friends and family.

Derm Kennedy and his wife Susanne have been outdoor enthusiasts all of their adult lives. Derm's retirement in 2003, after more than thirty years of employment with BCTel (Telus), provided the freedom and flexibility for them to continue their passion for the mountains and waters throughout Western Canada. Their recent outdoor adventures include kayaking: Vancouver to Prince Rupert in seven weeks, Prince Rupert to Juneau, Alaska in five weeks as well as several extended trips at Haida Gwaii, the magical archipelago on BC's North Coast.

Big Surprise

By Wendy Squire (Prince George, BC)

Perhaps it was having to be indoors so much that sparked my early and lifelong love of the outdoors.

I was a thin, pale, wide-eyed toddler and small for my age. Most of my earliest memories are of hospitals as that's where I spent too much time. It took years for the doctors to figure out what was wrong and fix it. In the hospital, I liked to be in the open courtyard or look out my window and imagine I was outside. If I leaned against the window, five floors up, I could look across the busy parking lot to a grassy hill with a tall pole. Perched on the pole was a real live go-kart. I'd imagine myself in the little racecar flying off the pole and racing anywhere. Pavement, grass, gravel, nothing slowed me down. No walls. Outside air. Free. I'd race up and down the soapbox track, across the grass, around the hospital parking lot, beside the road, over bumps and around trees...

Of course not all of my time was in the hospital, most of it was at home. Dolls and stuffed animals weren't important to me since I didn't like pretending an inanimate object was alive.

At home, I loved spending time outside. The back section of our property was steep and thick with trees and underbrush. The rest was a wide strip of lawn that sloped down to the gravel road. I liked our yard, lots of grass and lots of dirt. Dad loved the outdoors. He was a natural teacher who enjoyed sharing and explaining to me what he saw: the individual trees and bushes, the squirrels and birds, and how the sunlight played with the shadows.

I'm sure that's what prompted my parents to plan the surprise for us. They waited for everything to be just right and when the time came, my brother Ed and I were allowed to stay up late. The special surprise moment would be just before our unusually late bedtime.

I was about three and a half years old then so my typical bedtime was before the sun went down, but not that night. It was dark outside, especially where we lived on the outskirts of town. Our house was the second home on the west side of a dead end road. Across from us was a big sandy field edged with blueberry bushes and spruce trees. The road crossed the side of a hill overlooking a major highway heading north out of town; there were no streetlights and our road housed only a dozen neighbours.

It wasn't very often that my brother and I looked forward to bedtime but on this night we made no protests when it finally arrived. We had to be completely ready for bed: toys put away, teeth brushed, faces washed and pyjamas on. We had the best PJs – Grandma made them for us. They were soft, thick flannel with little pictures on them, like clowns or kittens. Dressed in our PJs, we were ready for our surprise.

Mom and Dad wrapped us in warm blankets and turned off the lights as we all went outside. Because it was early autumn the air had a chilly edge so the blankets were a good idea but it wouldn't have mattered because we were so excited. I had no idea what the surprise would be.

(My brother Ed and I and Crabbit, the cat)

We walked out onto the driveway, our footsteps and shadows soft on the hard packed dirt, the night air still and inviting. Ed toddled along with Mom while I stayed beside Dad. We stopped beside our red Volkswagen station wagon.

"Are you ready?" they asked.

We didn't get into the car. No one else was around and we were just standing there between the station wagon and our dark house. "Ready for what?"

"Look up!"

The sky was glowing! Only the edges were dark, everywhere else was overflowing with pricks of white lights, hundreds and hundreds and hundreds of them. Not just a few stars here and there but so many clustered together that the dots blurred together into bunches of light; different sizes that went on and on, as far as I could see and farther. So many stars that the black sky was blue. It was amazing, fantastic and wonderful.

"The Milky Way," Dad's soft, deep voice explained.

I didn't understand that he was telling me the name of the great collection of stars

I was seeing. Milk was stored in the fridge and I couldn't figure what he was telling me or why he suddenly switched topics.

The sky was different from other nights; it wasn't just bright dots here and there with lots of black sky in between. With so many stars there was almost no sky. I was awestruck.

I tapped on Dad's leg. When he looked down I lifted my arms and he scooped me up. Strangely, the stars weren't any closer. I reached up high toward the sky. The stars were still too far away. I was very surprised. I knew my world was bigger than my house and I'd learned it was bigger than my neighbourhood but that night I found out that however big my world was, it was just a small part of a really big, BIG.

Wendy Squire was born and raised in the heart of British Columbia and pursued a career as a Registered Nurse in northern Alberta. It wasn't long before she returned to BC and settled in the Okanagan. Nearly a quarter century later, Wendy moved back to Prince George. She enjoys writing fiction and non-fiction stories as well as scripts for stage and screen. Her interests include a love for the outdoors, carving, drawing and photography. She almost always has a cat or two, and a secret stash of dark chocolate.

PRIZE WINNER

By Darlene Foster (Orihuela Costa, Spain)

We were close to being a perfect family and we didn't need anyone else to disrupt things. Mom, good at family planning, spaced the three of us out evenly. Three years apart seemed just right, as far as I was concerned. A sister would have been nice. But in spite of the fact that little brothers could be annoying, I felt happy with the way things turned out.

I was not happy when I heard another baby was about to join our family. At almost sixteen, I didn't relish the idea of looking after a little kid and missing out on parties and fun stuff. Why did mom have to have another baby? Couldn't she be more responsible and think of the rest of us? Besides, wasn't she too old to be lugging around a small child? Angry at this turn of events, I decided not to speak to her ever again.

Mom explained that she hadn't planned this and it disrupted her life too. "Things don't always turn out the way we want but we have to accept them and make the best of the situation," she said.

I didn't care how Mom felt and refused to look up from my book as she spoke. My life was about to be ruined.

Mom looked awfully tired at times, and although I was not speaking to her, I tried to do as many of her chores as I could. I had a packed schedule with school, choir practise, drama club and Canadian Girls in Training. There'd be no time for the extra work a new baby in the house would entail. What if the child cried and I couldn't do my homework or study for exams? Could we even afford another mouth to feed?

February arrived, soon time for the annual Valentines Day dance at school—and I had nothing to wear! Mom had a piece of burgundy baby-wide corduroy in her sewing chest and we bought a Chanel style suit pattern the last time we were in town. She promised to have the suit made for the dance. After doing all the farm chores and cooking meals, she was always too tired to start the project. I would die if I had to wear something old to the dance. We had no money for a store bought dress.

Besides being a good seamstress, Mom was a great cook and baked mouth watering desserts. She often entered her recipes in contests, attended the bake offs and won prizes. That year she entered her Apple Cottage Cheese Pie recipe in the Medicine Hat News Recipe Contest. She passed her love of baking and cooking on to me and we enjoyed trying different recipes together. Once I entered a recipe contest and won a Five Roses Cook Book for honourable mention.

Mom also taught me to sew long before I took Home Economics in high school. I had already made a few things for myself: a shift dress, a couple of pop tops and a pair of shorts. By the time I took Home Economics, the obligatory pot holder and apron were a piece of cake for me. I ended up assisting the others with their sewing projects which was much appreciated by the overworked teacher.

The new baby was due mid February. Mom finally cut the suit out of the corduroy and assured me it would be completed for the Valentine's Dance. During the night of February 9, Dad woke us up to say he was taking Mom to the hospital as the baby was coming—and would I look after my brothers.

I mumbled, "Sure," while I snuggled deeper under the warm quilt.

My third brother was born on February 10. Dad reported mother and baby doing well. The news didn't have much effect on me except that Mom would not be home until after the dance, and she had barely started on the suit.

I moved the sewing machine out of my parent's bedroom into mine, studied the fabric pieces and sewing instructions, and with much care, made the A-line skirt. I admired the finished product in the mirror. It fit just right and actually looked store bought. I had never made anything as difficult as a jacket. I followed the instructions to a T and took my time. After a couple of frustrating hours fitting the sleeves so they were smooth, the jacket was finished—the night before the dance. Even the button holes looked good.

I felt like Jackie Kennedy in that suit. I received many compliments and didn't sit out one dance. My town friends, in store bought dresses, asked me if I could make them a suit just like it. It was my shining hour.

There was still the issue of a new person soon to inhabit our already crowded home, and I was not looking forward to it. They better not think I would babysit or help out in any way because I just wouldn't. I had too much to do already. This baby wasn't my concern.

I began to put things away in Mom's sewing chest and considered sewing myself something else after the success of the suit. Mom had lots of pieces of material that she never got around to sewing. In my search through the fabric I came across a large piece of canary yellow flannelette and a package of baby patterns.

An idea started to form. The sewing machine was still in my bedroom and it would be a couple more days until mom came home. I spent the entire weekend sewing a baby bunting bag for my new little brother. It turned out so cute. I looked forward to seeing him in it.

On Sunday I gave the house a good cleaning since Mom was coming home the next day. First she had to go the Medicine Hat News office to collect her prize for the Apple Cottage Cheese Pie recipe and get her picture taken. Dad took the dress she requested when he went to pick her up from the hospital. He also took the bunting bag.

Dad, Mom and baby arrived home soon after we got home from school. Mom beamed as she handed me a cute little person in a canary yellow, flannelette bunting bag. "Thanks for making this for your little brother."

I held the precious bundle and fell in love. We had lots of room in our house and our hearts for this little guy. He would be fun to look after.

The following weekend Mom's picture appeared in the Medicine Hat News. With a big smile, Mom held her prize winning pie in front of her. No one could tell she had just had a baby and could not do up the zipper in the back of her dress.

Mom may have won an electric frying pan for her prize winning recipe but I got the best prize—my wonderful little brother!

(1970 photo of my three brothers & dad on the family farm; Insert: My mom and I in 2010)

Brought up on a ranch in southern Alberta, **Darlene Foster** (www.darlenefoster.ca) dreamt of travelling the world and meeting interesting people. She had a desire to write since she was twelve. Her short stories have won a number of awards. She is the author of the exciting adventure series featuring spunky 12 year-old Amanda Ross who loves to travel to unique places. Her books include: Amanda in Arabia; The Perfume Flask, Amanda in Spain; The Girl in The Painting, Amanda in England; The Missing Novel and Amanda in Alberta; and The Writing on the Stone. Readers of all ages enjoy travelling with Amanda as she unravels one mystery after another. Darlene and her husband divide their time between the west coast of Canada and Orihuela Costa, in Spain. She was encouraged by her parents to follow her dreams, and believes everyone is capable of making their dreams come true.

All the Fun of the Fair

赶 庙 会

By Francisco Little (Beijing, China)

Someone shoved me in the back while I was trying to figure out what exactly was being cooked in the huge vat of boiling oil. Scorpions, fried to a crisp on long skewers. I couldn't stop long, the crowd just wouldn't allow it.

It wasn't the noise so much as the feeling of being in a strait jacket and moving involuntarily in a human tidal wave of thousands. If nothing else being shoulder to shoulder helped to keep warm in the subzero temperature.

In Beijing, Spring Festival just isn't Spring Festival without a visit to a Temple Fair. It's an ideal way to dive into Chinese folk culture and enjoy the carnival atmosphere with all the bargaining of a market. But it's not an outing for the faint-hearted.

Having been around for at least a thousand years, some fairs have kept their traditional link with religious rituals during Chinese New Year. In Ditan Park (Temple of Earth) people rush blindly to the centre of the park, clutching three incense sticks and bowing elaborately three times before the fire at the altar. It was the place where in days gone by only the Emperor would stand, as he offered his sacrifice to the God of the Earth for blessings on the Middle Kingdom.

"I don't really believe in these religious rituals as they are just some kind of superstition," said my friend Li Yong Mei. However, saying that didn't stop her from scrambling up to the altar to ask for fortune in the year ahead.

"For just in case," she smiled. Better safe than sorry right?

Right.

(Local Beijing snacks are a major attraction - Photo Credit, Francisco Little)

Near the altar a performer was hitting all the high notes in a Peking Opera recital, while dancers on long wooden stilts floated high among the crowds. Onwards, ever onwards. As we moved I almost had my face squashed against the protruding plump bum cheeks of a toddler riding on her Dad's shoulders. She was wearing a pair of those ventilated trousers that have easy access for toilet functions. The little cheeks were apple red, seemingly frozen on such a chilly morning.

An entire goat on a spit, Mongolians stripped to the waist in cowboy hats tempting the crowds with their skewered lamb, a woman smacking squid to flatten it against a sizzling grill — the air swam with spice laden smoke. This was snack central. People made small islands in amongst the flowing mass munching on an unimaginable variety of snacks, silent for a brief gastronomical moment. The ground was a trellis of dumped wooden skewers. I was busy slurping my sesame porridge when I saw Li waving me over.

"Come and look at this guy," she shouted above the din. I pushed my way over to where a vendor was creating animals out of sugar, using a glass-blowing technique. He sat seemingly unperturbed, warming up the toffee. Then, taking a small lump he blew, pulled and tweaked until it magically resembled a bull, reminding us all that this was indeed the Chinese year of the Ox. People snapped up the bulls as fast as he could make them.

I finished my porridge just as an excited vendor wearing a pink wig and yellow goggles waved one of those ubiquitous multicolored windmills in my face and tried to sell me a face mask and a rubber snake. I never did work out the connection.

I stretched my hand high up above the hordes and snapped pictures as I bobbed and weaved in the Temple Fair shuffle. Somehow the wave had moved us to what looked like a planet made entirely of soft toys. Teddy bears, pandas, oxes and even crocodiles. Some were strung from beams by their necks, causing a crying fit from a small girl near me who thought the toys were being punished.

I tried my hand at one of the traditional games throwing a small hoop over protruding tubes. The attendant had shown me the hoop did in fact fit over. Having

long arms I was able to stretch across and almost drop the hoops over the tubes. The attendants exchanged glances, went into a huddle, debated, then nodded and handed over one of the large bears that had previously hung in the gallows. Shouts of 'Hao, Hao (bravo, bravo)!' went up from the crowd.

Around me the park hung thick with red lanterns, and I needed to step back and find a place of refuge. I was sideswiped into a small clearing which seemed to offer some escape, but just then a troupe of carriers dressed in red outfits danced past, an ancient sedan chair on their shoulders. Perched on the chair a happy child laughed her head off as she was bounced along, while Mom ran alongside trying to take as many pictures of her pride and joy as was humanly possible.

There was no getting away from the action. Li was calling again. "Come on, come on," she said, "this is not the time to relax." I guess it wasn't, and dived back into the fray.

(Temple Fair celebrations – Photo Credit, Francisco Little)

Francisco Little (www.instagram. com/franciscophotography/) is a much traveled South African born writer, photographer and artist, who grew up Rhodesia, now Zimbabwe, where he studied Fine Art and Philosophy. He currently works as managing editor of a current affairs magazine and resides in Beijing, China.

DON MESSER'S *Violin*

By GARY DOI (Penticton, BC)

Don Messer

Sometimes life brings things together in ways so unexpected and joyful. A fortunate happenstance . . . I'm not sure what else to call it.

In 1998 my wife, two children and I were living in Port Hardy, British Columbia, the most northern town on Vancouver Island. I was the Superintendent of Schools for the small school district, which encompassed a large geographic region.

One day, the district's Fine Arts Coordinator phoned.

"Frank Leahy, the National Fiddle Champion from Ontario, is in town today touring the schools," he said. "He needs a place to stay. The home previously arranged didn't work out as they have cats. Frank is allergic to cats. I was wondering if you'd

take him in?"

"No problem. He can stay with my family," I said. "Tell Mr. Leahy I'm not a cat person either."

He chuckled. Then as a footnote he added, "By the way, Frank Leahy recently inherited Don Messer's violin."

"Really?" I said. "Now, how interesting is that?"

After the call ended, I sat for a few moments thinking about the once famous TV personality Don Messer. I recall watching Don Messer's Jubilee almost every week in 1960. That was the year we first purchased a television set, a brand new twenty-one inch black and white Zenith console. I was about ten years old at the time.

I remember the "Rabbit Ears," a v-shaped antenna on top of the television. That's how

we captured the signal to two channels: CBC and KXLY. The weather often interfered with the reception but I still watched, rain or shine. Don Messer's Jubilee was a popular variety show in Canada back then. Each program opened with his signature song—"Goin' to the Barn Dance Tonight".

And now, the man who owned Don Messer's violin was coming to stay at my place.

Frank Leahy was a wonderful house guest. One of my daughters, a violin student, showed him her instrument, which had been passed down through the generations from her grandfather. Frank examined it, played a little song and commented on the warm sound quality. He then brought out Don Messer's violin and entertained us with some lively East Coast fiddling. It was like watching a master at work.

"What a responsibility it must be to own that instrument," I said to Frank.

"It certainly is," he said. "Don Messer's daughter gave her father's violin to me as she wanted the instrument to be played. I also received rights to the Don Messer name and image."

We talked further about his tour and other events he had planned across the country. At one point Frank asked if I knew of a special place on the Northwest Coast for a school performance.

That's when I told him about Hartley Bay, home of the Gitga'at Nation. Located at the mouth of Douglas Channel about 400 miles north of Vancouver, BC, the isolated First Nations fishing village (population 200) was accessible only by air and water. They had boardwalks instead of roadways and an elementary school that was the pride of the village.

Frank was interested so I wrote a letter of introduction to School Principal Ernie Hill. I had worked with Ernie years before and knew he would warmly welcome Frank to the school and community.

We said our goodbyes the next morning as Frank was off to visit other schools and communities.

And that was it. Or, so I thought.

Six months passed.

One day, as I was driving down the Vancouver Island highway, I heard Frank Leahy on CBC radio discussing the release of his new album. Near the end of the program, the interviewer asked the question: Of all the places on your tour, was there one place that really stood out?

"Yes, there was," Frank said. "It was a village called Hartley Bay."

I immediately pulled over to the side of the road to listen.

After performing for an appreciative school audience,

Frank Leahy

(Hartley Bay, BC)

Frank said he went outside to enjoy the beauty of the natural environment. While he was standing there, a native elder approached him and introduced herself. She had heard about the school concert.

"Do you know the Don Messer song 'The Honeymoon Waltz'?" the woman asked.

"I do," said Frank. "Although it's been a while since I played it."

"Well, my husband and I danced to it at our wedding many, many years ago," she explained. "My husband recently passed away and I'd love to hear that song again."

Frank told her he'd be pleased to play the song. Even more, he told her he would play it on the violin that Don Messer himself used on his show.

She lifted her head and looked at Frank.

"You have Don Messer's violin?" she asked, her eyes wide.

Frank nodded and reached for his case. He clicked open the latches, took out the precious instrument and raised the violin to his shoulder. He drew the bow gently across the strings and began to play.

The warm breeze carried the slow, tender melodic sounds amongst the tall cedars and throughout the little village. The music captivated her. She closed her eyes but could not hold back the tears.

Interview over, I sat in my car trying to soak in what I had just heard. In an isolated fly-in coastal village, a native elder asked fiddler Frank Leahy to play a special Don Messer song as a remembrance to her late husband. To the woman's surprise and delight, Frank Leahy did that and more—he performed it on Don Messer's violin.

Now, how special is that?

(**Hartley Bay Cultural Centre**; Photo credit: Lynne Hill)

Gary Doi has served as a superintendent of schools, teacher, consultant, school administrator and university lecturer. In retirement he has dedicated much of my time inspiring hope through stories. To this end, Gary has published and marketed four anthologies—One Story at a Time; Fly Like an Eagle; From the Heart; and In the Moment. All proceeds from book sales benefit charities. In addition to his volunteer work, Gary continues to pursue his interests in golf, mountain biking, photography and travel.

CHRISTMAS with Family

By Leanne Dyck (Mayne Island, BC)

November wasn't even over and already the rush had begun. My neighbourhood mall was packed. Everyone had a shopping bag. Some carried two. I sped past shop after shop escorted by Christmas tunes. *Deck the halls with lots of presents. Fa, la, la, la, la, la, la, la, la. Now's the time to be shopping. Fa, la, la, la, la, la, la, la, la..* The music was supposed to make me happy, but all I felt was blue.

I pictured my extended family's Christmas Eve celebration. Year after year, we gathered to talk, laugh, exchange gifts and enjoy delicious food. This year, they would—I wouldn't, not any longer. My husband and I had moved from Manitoba three provinces away to British Columbia.

I entered the food court, searched and found my husband, Byron, sitting at a table, flipping through a magazine. "I'm sorry I'm late," I said. Byron doesn't like to wait.

He shrugged off my apology.

The thought of spending Christmas here in BC—the two of us alone in our lonely apartment—made me want to cry.

"I want us to go home for Christmas," I said trying to steady my voice.

"We are home," he replied.

"No, I mean—"

"Manitoba? Freezing cold. Snow. No thanks."

But we have to be with family for Christmas. That thought haunted me all the way back to our apartment. *I know, I'll phone my cousin Susan. After all she's alone too.*

"Why don't you and Byron come and have Christmas here on Salt Spring?" Susan suggested.

I was so happy I wanted to sing, dance, but all I did was thank my cousin for saving my Christmas.

Weeks later, I was at the breakfast table listening to the radio.

"We're guaranteed to have a white Christmas this year," the weatherman predicted.

"What does he know? It's all guesswork."

Byron waved his hand to silence me.

"Tons of snow will make traveling hazardous," the weatherman concluded.

"I think we should postpone our trip to Salt Spring. Our sports car isn't equipped for driving up snow-covered hills. We can always visit Susan later when the weather's better," Byron said.

"No we have to…" My voice choked. "It's Christmas. We need to be with family."

He patted my hand. "We'll try."

Days before it was necessary, I made reservations with the ferry that would take us from the Mainland to Salt Spring. Time trickled by until finally the day came.

I eased out of bed, crept over to the window, breathed out slowly, crossed my fingers and pushed back the curtains. A light dusting of snow covered the ground. Large, fluffy snowflakes continued to fall. *It looks so pretty, just like C-h-r-i-s-t-m-a-s… No! We have to…*

Byron rolled over and faced me. "How's it look?"

I pulled the curtains together. "Fine. Just fine."

He crawled out of bed and pushed back the curtains. "I think we should phone Susan and cancel."

"No, we can't. It's Christmas. It'll ease up. I know it will."

He snorted. "So now you're a weather forecaster?"

"Please, we have to try."

Grumbling, Byron loaded our luggage into our car and drove us to the ferry.

A short line of cars lead to the ticket booth. The BC Ferry worker slid back the window. "Are you sure you—"

"Yes, we're sure." *We can't be alone. It's Christmas. We need to be with family.*

Another BC Ferry worker directed us onto the ferry, but not before saying, "Are you sure you—"

I cut him off too.

We boarded the ferry. A routine two-hour trip ended up taking eight hours as we were diverted and re-diverted. But eventually we docked at Salt Spring Island.

"You see we made it," I said, trying to be cheerful.

Byron fixed me with steel eyes. "The ferry was only half the battle. The other half is that steep hill." He pointed with his chin.

"But…but you said we would try."

"Yes, Leanne. I did." By the way he said my name I knew he'd lost his Christmas cheer.

"You're a good driver. I have faith in you."

Byron did try. He cranked his neck to peer out the side window and turned the steering wheel. We started to slide. He cranked his neck the other way to peer out that window. We began to fish-tail; he turned the steering wheel and kept us on the road, barely. Then he started the whole neck thing again. He looked like he was watching a tennis match. Over and over again, he tried, but the farthest he got was halfway up the hill.

I closed my eyes and visualized my three brothers pushing us up that hill. "This time you'll make it," I heard them promise. But they weren't there; Bryon and I were alone. I forced back tears.

Byron yanked the gear shift into park and glared at me. "You got any more brilliant ideas?" He asked after driving backwards over that three-mile steep, curving hill. "We could be safe and warm in our apartment. But no you had to drag us all the way out here. And now… And now… It's pitch black. We're stuck in a blizzard. And we don't know anyone who can help us. Happy?"

No, I wasn't happy. I'd gotten us into this mess; I had to get us out. I typed Susan's number into my cellphone.

"I'd go and get you myself but my Toyota doesn't like snow. I'm afraid I'd only end up stranded too. Try a tow truck or a taxi?" She gave me the numbers. The tow truck driver's voice mail message wished me a Merry Christmas. The taxi driver laughed in my ear. Byron was beginning to swear which I had to admit was justified.

Desperate, I phoned Susan again.

"Hitchhike," she said.

"What?"

"Ask for a ride. Someone will help you."

By the tone of her voice I knew she was serious. She wanted me to ask a complete stranger for help. Clearly she hadn't watched those horror movies I had; I knew what would happen if I followed her advice— Byron and I would be abducted or worse.

What's that noise? I looked over at Byron. *Are his teeth chattering?*

I have to do something. But what? We're a steep hill away from Susan, a hotel, a restaurant—almost everything. I looked across the street. Everything but that grocery store.

Three large trucks with snow tires were parked in front of the store.

"I'll be right back." I unclipped my seat belt.

"Wait. Where are you going?"

"To the grocery store." I opened the door. "I'm going to ask for a ride."

"What? You can't. We don't know any—"

I closed the car door on the rest of his sentence.

Large sleigh bells jiggled as I walked into the store. The sound made me think of Christmas angels. I said a silent prayer, "Please, this has to work."

I surveyed the store—not for groceries— for an angel. A few aisles away a woman was talking with a teenager who I thought must be her daughter. "Please, can you help? My cousin is expecting me for Christmas but my car won't climb the hill."

"Of course," she said, "I'd be happy to."

And just like that, our problem was solved. She made room in her truck for our luggage, Bryon and me. And she drove us right to my cousin's door.

There I had a merry Christmas with family.

Leanne and Byron's Christmas adventure made them dream of island life. They did some island hopping and fell in love with Mayne Island. Leanne's writing is inspired by the beauty she finds there. Since 2010, **Leanne Dyck** has been published in seven magazines, through a small press and in three anthologies. Please visit Leanne on-line: www.leannedyck.com and http://authorleannedyck.blogspot.ca

(Salt Spring Snow Storm, Photo Credit: John Cameron)

Memory from Childhood

By Danell Clay (Prince George, BC)

Back in the seventies, I lived on the edge of Prince George's city limits. There was a dirt road and plenty of greenbelt and only two kids that lived on the block. Matt probably wished there was another nine-year old boy with whom he could have shared slingshot practice, but instead he had me, a girl who liked to read and who turned everything into a story. He was serious and I wasn't.

He seemed to feel that it was only a matter of time before I became lost in the woods so he tried teaching survival skills which I generally ignored. One day, the two of us were toolie-tromping in the forest out back of his house. Matt used his pocket knife to scrape off a glob of half-dried pitch from the trunk of a pine.

"It's like chewing-gum," he said, offering it to me still on the knife blade.

"Looks like poison," I said.

Matt popped it into his mouth.

"When you have to walk a long way in the woods, chewing on this can keep you going." I tried it and the pitch tasted like a tree smells, which wasn't horrible but wasn't Double-Bubble either. I ran my hands along the grey tree-trunk, smooth except for bubbles like blisters under skin. I used a twig to pop one of the blisters and fresh sap flowed from the wound.

"We are chewing tree blood," I said making my voice sound ghoulish and holding my hands in front of me like claws. I had sap on one hand and it was sticky as syrup but wiping it on my pants didn't help one bit. In fact, dirt seemed to be magnetized to both my hand and the spot just above my knee, both were becoming blacker by the minute. It didn't help that I soon had it smeared across my face. Matt seemed to take my rapidly deteriorating appearance for granted.

"See those ferns? You can eat them too, but not now, early on when they are just coming out of the ground. You know what they look like in the spring?"

"They look curly, like commas or a strip of paper you wind on a pencil or..."

"You can boil the fiddleheads and eat them like spinach." He lost my interest at the word 'spinach'. I found it difficult to imagine the horrifying circumstance that would reduce me to eating ferns. Instead of listening, I gathered the moss that clung to branches like matted green thread.

"The moss is called 'old man's beard'" said Matt, 'and it makes a great fire-starter." To illustrate, he located a tree with a hollow at the base of its roots. "You need to keep the fire protected from the wind." He broke a few dry branches and placed them in the hollow. He made a small nest of the moss and placed strips of dry bark on top. Then, from a pocket, he produced a block of flint and struck it with a chunk of steel. The spark landed in the dry bark and he blew gently until a flame flickered into life. He transferred the fire-starter into the root-hollow. At one point, he threw a hunk of pitch in the fire and it popped and hissed while the flame changed color.

"It's like a witches' oven," I said. The fire caught the branches and leapt higher.

"Marshmallows!" I suggested.

"Put it out! It's too big." We kicked dirt and stomped on the branches.

"Matt, there's still smoke coming from up there," I pointed above our heads at a crack in the tree. He knelt to check the hollow in the tree's roots.

"The tree was hollow all the way up and a spark started burning inside. I need to get my parents."

"But you'll get in trouble! How long is your garden hose? What if we had a bucket of water and a ladder?" Matt brushed the dirt from his knees with resignation and started trudging towards his house to tell his mom and dad. I watched him go. There was crackling inside the tree and the bark was warm. Smoke and sparks billowed into the sky.

Phone calls were made, sirens blared and a team of firefighters jumped from the truck. They used a chainsaw to fall the tree and section it. Matt reassured the fire captain that it would never happen again.

There was a lesson in that burning tree, about making mistakes but facing the consequences and about shouldering responsibilities. As I watched Matt accept the blame for the fire without making excuses, he was finally able to teach me something.

Danell Clay is a long-time resident of Prince George, BC, where she works as a library technician in a small medical library. Books are one of her favorite vices. She attends a writing group and has been dared to write 50,000 words in the month of November, as part of the National Novel Writing Month (NaNoWriMo).

THE PHOTOGRAPHER BEAR

(Kootenay Reflections; Photo Credit: Jim Lawrence)

Moments of Insight

"Sometimes you never know the value
of a moment until it becomes a memory."
Dr. Seuss

"Great Bear Anchorage"
— Roy Henry Vickers

Rainbow Alley

By Roy Henry Vickers (Hazelton, BC)

"Rainbow Alley" is a legendary stretch of water in northern British Columbia where Babine Lake flows into Nilkitkwa Lake. The name comes from the large rainbow trout that live there. In June of each year, huge hatches of stoneflies spark a feeding frenzy creating near perfect conditions for fly fishing enthusiasts.

We were staying in a beautiful cabin by the water's edge. I was there with my two sons and a lifelong friend who loved fly fishing and custom fly-tying.

I rise early, usually well before others. This morning when I got up though, my son Wakas was not in the cabin. I went outside on the porch and looked about. That's when I saw him. He was on the dock, fishing in the peace and quiet. Wakas understood that getting up before the sun can pay huge dividends with trout fishing.

Smoke from a forest fire far away gave a soft amber glow to the eastern sky and reflected its warm orange radiance on the water. In the distance, the eerie call of a loon echoed across the still waters.

I thought of the wonders of such a moment in the mind of a boy. How would Wakas remember his time at the lake? Was it something that would stay with him for years to come?

Watching him reminded me of my own childhood over sixty years ago in the coastal Tsimshian village of Kitkatla, British Columbia. I have rich memories of family, friends and the natural environment.

I remember one summer in the village when all my school friends had gone to work in fish canneries at the mouth of the Skeena River. Lonely and bored, I often visited Mrs. Spencer, an old woman who lived near my home. I called her "grandmother" even though she wasn't really my grandmother. She'd invite me to sit with her by the warmth of the wood stove.

Grandmother couldn't speak English and I couldn't speak the Tsimshian language, but that didn't seem to matter. She sat in her chair humming a song. In silence, I'd watch the rhythmic action of her hands as she weaved a cedar basket. I felt comfort, care and love, just by being there. Old Helen Spencer taught me it is okay to be silent and communicate with emotions.

As I grew older I spent a lot of my summer on the water with my grandpa Henry. My job was to watch the gill net and observe whether the corks or floats were bobbing, an indicator that salmon were caught in the mesh.

One morning while on "watch duty" I heard what sounded like rifle shots. I rushed below deck to wake Grandpa who was still asleep as he had worked through the night.

"Grandpa! Grandpa!" I called out. "Someone is shooting."

"Shooting?" asked Grandpa, rubbing his eyes. He rose from the bed, listened for a few seconds and then shook his head.

"Killer whales," he calmly declared.

Not long after, a super pod of 100 or so whales came through, jumping and playing two at a time and in singles, slapping their tails on the water's surface with such force it actually sounded like gunshots. After the whales left, the fishing boats in the area pulled up their nets and started to leave. My grandpa, however, had other ideas. He moved his boat closer to shore and reset his gill net along the kelp beds.

When the net was set, Grandpa just stood and watched and waited. It wasn't long before the whole net—all 50 or 60 yards of it—started to sink. So many fish hit the net coming out of the kelp patch that he had to radio for help from other gill-netters.

"How did you know the salmon were there?" I asked Grandpa after all the fish had been loaded and shared amongst the fishermen.

"Oh, the fish found a hiding spot," he replied, his smile wide. "Sockeye don't just disappear. They had to go somewhere."

So, I learned from my grandpa that everything isn't always what it seems.

'Pay attention. Think like a fish,' he'd say to me.

Another time Grandpa and I were pulling some logs behind a rowboat. It was difficult rowing so we took turns working the oars. As we approached the village the church bells rang. I remember smiling to myself because I had an excuse not to go to church. But even then, I braced for another scolding from Granny.

"Grandpa, how come you never go to church?" I asked.

Grandpa shook his head, blew out a long breath. His eyes shot skyward. Then he looked about from side-to-side as we kept rowing. I wondered what he was doing or looking at so I began to look around as well.

"This is my church," Grandpa said raising his arms high in the air. "I go every day."

Those early memories have endured over the years. How to survive, get your food, keep your house warm. How to care for Mother Earth and respect her gifts. How to listen, share and give back.

And yes, how to think like a fish.

Something Walkus was learning that very moment. There was a strong tug and the water came alive. A gleaming rainbow broke the surface with a tail-dance and then raced across the current into an eddy. The battle was on.

Welcome to Rainbow Alley in June.

(Rainbow Alley – Painting by Roy Henry Vickers)

In the Moment — Real Life Stories of Hope and Inspiration

Canadian artist **Roy Henry Vickers** is a world-renowned printmaker, painter, carver, author and designer whose signature style fuses the traditional images of his West Coast native ancestry with the realism of his British heritage. His artwork is held in museums and private collections across Canada and internationally, and is sold through his successful artist-owned and operated gallery. In addition Roy is a recognized leader in the First Nations community, and a tireless spokesperson for recovery from addictions and abuse.

Pedaling Progress

By Aimee Ledewitz Weinstein (Washington, DC)

"Go! Go!" I screamed, "You're doing it! You're doing it!" I put my hands in the pockets of my red, zippered sweatshirt and watched my son wobble down the street on the bicycle without training wheels for the first time. Twenty seconds later, he put his feet down, turned to look at me, and the width of the grin on his face, with the huge, indented dimples in each cheek was stopped only by his ears.

"Bailey! Bailey is on the bike!" Behind me, my two-year-old daughter was on her own bike equipped with training wheels, standing perfectly still.

"Keep going!" I hollered down the street toward my son.

"I can't; I can't start." Bailey said, his five-year-old eyebrows furrowing.

I jogged toward him, leaving Sydney behind me to do her shuffle-pedal that got her forward inch by inch. She didn't yet understand the around-and-around-mo-tion of pedaling and moved her feet back and forth on the pedals.

I held Bailey's bike steady while he scrambled on it and settled himself. With one push, he was off and I ran back to Sydney, pushing her forward without the benefit of her own motion to follow Bailey around the corner.

We were lucky; the weather was holding. It was overcast and only about 65 degrees, unusually cold for mid-May in Tokyo. We were near Hundred-Yen park, and the National Stadium, where baseball reigns supreme. Every Sunday the city closes the streets around the area and loans out bikes to anyone who wants to ride on the mile long circular course. This was the perfect option for our city-bred children.

All eyes seemed to be on my children as we cycled around the course. In a city of almond-eyes and uniformly black, straight hair, my kids stand out with their blond locks, Sydney's in a mass of out-of-control curls.

The morning had been quiet for us and because my husband in the States on business, the children had been extra good for me. As an expat in Asia, I lived for messages from home, and the first thing that I had done that morning was check email. There was a message from the head of my dissertation committee that he and the other two committee members had finally been

through my first draft after nine weeks of having it. The news wasn't good. While they didn't feel that I needed to do more research with my students, the entire work needed massive additions and corrections – a true re-focusing.

I allowed myself five minutes of frustrated tears. I had spent the month of February finishing the draft. On most weekends I had worked during the day for part of both days.

"Can't you spend the whole day with us today, Mom? It's Saturday." Bailey often pointed out. I agonized. I wanted to get the thing done, but I didn't want to hurt my kids. For the hundredth time since

starting the dissertation process, I wondered what had possessed me to have children before finishing the doctorate. I was only thirty-three; it's not like time was running out on my fertility.

I read my director's three pages of comments once carefully. Thankfully, the committee had met and agreed on one set of comments to make instead of sending me individual and confusing feedback. I also knew that when I was feeling less emotional about it, I would find their comments useful. My doctorate is in English education and I am a writer, so I know that drafts are part of the territory. I generally have tough skin with criticism, after the first five minutes of devastation. I also knew that my draft was unfocused and that I needed some specific suggestions on how to move it forward toward a cohesive whole.

But because my husband was away, I didn't have the luxury of going through the commentary a second time right then. The kids were relying on me to take them cycling, as I had promised.

Since coming to Tokyo two years prior for my husband's work as an attorney, I had been lucky enough to find work at Temple University, Japan, a branch campus of Temple's Philadelphia campus. I taught freshman composition and research writing and directed their Learning Center. My kids went to school and we had a fantastic Filipina nanny to round out the rough edges of child and home-care.

One late afternoon over our first winter in Tokyo, I was standing near my desk at TUJ. Professors do not have offices, but sit in a large cube-farm, where each professor has a desk. I was preparing to see a student quickly before meeting my husband and a client for dinner. All of a sudden my phone rang and it was the nanny telling me that

Bailey & Sydney

the plumber was in the house but needed to see me urgently regarding our plugged-up toilet. As she was telling me this, the student walked in and looked at me expectantly while I was holding my telephone and standing in front of her wearing my fancy black suit, pearls and high heels for dinner.

I wasn't sure what to do first. "AAHHH," I screamed out reflexively, "My roles are crashing!"

The chuckles emanating from the other cubicles brought me crashing back to reality. Quickly, I rescheduled the student meeting for first thing in the morning, called my husband to tell him that I'd be slightly late for dinner, and rushed home to meet the plumber to consult on the status of our toilet before rushing back out again, completely disappointing the kids because I wasn't staying. That type of juggling defined my life.

The prospect of re-working the dissertation, classes starting for the summer term, and all of the things that had to get done weighed heavily on my brain as I was out with the kids with the bikes, though. Half of my mind was on the kids, while the other half was divided between the dissertation and my job and a smattering of chores such as paying for Bailey's "belt test" in his Aikido class and buying more insect repellant. Keeping track of the minutiae of life tended to get pushed to the edge. Bailey finished biking triumphantly, and we planned a celebratory ice cream. We were meeting friends for dinner only an hour later, but this accomplishment only comes along once in a boy's life.

Dinner, however, was a bit of a disaster. First, we decided to take the thirty minute walk to the restaurant and we were halfway through it before we realized but it was too late to turn back or catch a cab. I was tired, the kids were tired, and it was a terrible combination. When the kids did normal

kid-stuff, like run in circles on the sidewalk, or try to leave the table in the restaurant, I got more annoyed than necessary. It didn't help that we got home at 7:30pm, and the kids needed to get into bed quickly because it was a school night.

I showered them, and dispatched them to their rooms to get their pajamas on. I had to help Sydney, and I called out to Bailey that he had better be dressed when I finished with his sister – I would count to ten before coming into his room. Well, he started to wail at the top of his lungs. I ran into his room and found him sitting on his bed stark-naked. In all the time I had been dressing Sydney, he hadn't made a move toward dressing himself, and had instead been playing with his action figures. That really was my last nerve. I oversaw his dressing and put him to bed without a story, yelling that he was ungrateful for all of the nice things we had done that day. More tears, more wailing.

"I'm not a good boy!" he wept, but I ignored him and went to put Sydney to bed. I kissed her and sang her requested lullaby, breathing in the sweetness of her freshly washed hair and still-baby skin. It calmed me enough to go back to Bailey's room for a "snuggle" whereby I was able to hug and kiss him, albeit briefly.

I vegetated for the next hour in front of crap-TV, the only type of program available in Japan for English speakers in a pre-Netflix era.

Before going into my room to read and rest, I decided to close the door to Sydney's room. As I did it, I heard her whimpering: "It's too dark with the door closed."

I went in and knelt by her bed.

"Sing L'ailah Tov" she mumbled, naming her favorite Hebrew lullaby. Just the week before, Sydney had unwillingly given up her pacifier and now she was looking for some comfort. Pressing my

cheek to hers, I sang only the first few lines of the song softly. Her arm went slack against my neck and I could hear the regular sleep-pattern breathing. I bowed my head as I extricated myself from her. For how much longer would Mommy's voice comfort her like that?

Though I hadn't planned to, I went back into Bailey's room and knelt by his bed. His pillow was vertical, and I fixed it, repositioning him on the bed, but he never woke up.

It was at that moment that I felt the prick of tears behind my eyes, and with a sob, let them flow down my cheeks. The questions kept piling up on me one after the other. How was I going to be a good mother when I was working full time? How was I going to get my dissertation completed with all of my other responsibilities? Would I ever be able stop working and still have the strength and tolerance to be a good mother? How was I going to start teaching yet another semester in only two days when my syllabi weren't fully prepared? Why on earth couldn't I have more patience with my son and his normal, five-year-old shenanigans? And how was I ever going to teach Sydney to pedal properly if I always had to run after Bailey's bike?

I must have sat there on my knees for thirty minutes while my son slept soundly. I watched his little chest rise and fall. I wanted to do better. I wanted to do better for Bailey and for his sister.

In those moments in the dark as I cried, I realized that it didn't matter if my life was defined by juggling if that is what made me happy. The key lay in making the most of the time in each facet of my life. When I was with the kids, I had to be present in the moment. When I was at work, I had to try to keep my mind there. And somehow, I was going to have to muster the strength to re-work my entire dissertation to make it acceptable to my committee. If getting a doctorate was important to me, then that is what I would have to do. The kids would be no worse for the wear if I left them with their father on the weekends and wrote. If I got it done in a timely manner, they would never even remember the time I was not there.

It was not fair to anybody if I was taking a momentous occasion like Bailey's first bike ride and turning it into a stress-fest because I was focused only on my own schoolwork and other issues.

Bailey still didn't wake up as I kissed his cheek and smoothed the hair back from his face. I had to go into my room and reply to my professor's email, telling him that I got the suggestions and would get to work immediately on them.

Maybe Sydney didn't need to learn to pedal the right way just now. If the shuffle-pedal moved her along at her own preferred pace, and it made her happy, all that really mattered was the forward motion.

Maybe I should consider a shuffle-pedal of my own.

(Aimee Weinstein with her children Sydney and Bailey)

Dr. Aimee Weinstein (TokyoWriter. com) is a writer and writing professor who lived ten out of the last twelve years in Tokyo, Japan. She received her doctorate from the Department of Higher Education at George Mason University and has held positions at Temple University Japan, The George Washington University, and George Mason University. She has taught a variety of writing courses, from freshman composition to advanced expository writing. Her work has been published in Kaleidescope, Tokyo Weekender, inTouch, and Asian Jewish Life. She also maintains a regular blog where she fondly observes Tokyo life through the eyes of an American expat and writes about writing. Aimee currently resides in Washington D.C. with her supportive husband and two beautiful children, where she continues to write and help others in their writing.

UNLOCKING
MY VOICE

By Alison DeLory (Halifax, Nova Scotia)

The stranger's hand was around my neck. His index and middle fingers crawled up my chin, and when my jaw dropped in shock they slid over my bottom lip and across my tongue. I did not scream. I did not bite. I took it.

On this scorching summer day some years ago I had taken my two young children to play in Toronto's High Park. As we were leaving my eldest son, then five, pitched his rubber ball into a sparsely wooded area. It bounced and promptly disappeared.

"My ball! Where did it go?" he asked. In the oppressive humidity and despite our fatigue, we began searching for it. This area of woods is nestled inside High Park's circular drive, and though dotted with sky-scraping White Oak trees, there is plenty of open space through which you can see passing cars, cyclists and pedestrians on either side. A man walking through the same area asked if we wanted his help. My radar went up but in the presence of my children and in full sunlight I ignored my instincts and said okay.

We made it a game, stomping around in our sandals, kicking leaves and acorns aside as we peered amongst the roots for about 10 minutes, all with no luck. The ball seemed to have disappeared. I negotiated with my five-year-old who agreed it was time to give up. I grabbed my toddler's hand and we prepared to leave.

"Don't quit already. Come here miss," the man helping us beckoned. I contemplated bolting but I wasn't able to round up my kids quickly and besides, it felt like it would be an over-reaction. This man had given me no reason to fear him and he'd joined in our search game. Plus I didn't want my children to see me flee in response to the apparent kindness of a stranger. I wanted them to know there are helpful people in the world. I approached him.

"You have a beautiful neck," he told me. Strange, I thought, but not dangerous.

"Thanks. We have to go," I replied, pulling my kids tightly to my side.

"Wait," he implored. "It so long and so white. I love your neck." In a split second he had his hand around my throat. I lost my words. My body stiffened.

"And your mouth. Your mouth is so lovely." That's when he thrust his fingers between my lips. I stared at him, taking a mental picture. I noticed his hair colour, height, groomed beard, and slightly askew eye. But I didn't scream or bite or run. Joggers and people pushing strollers were visible in the distance. I could hear the happy squealing of children at the nearby splash-pad. I pulled my head backwards, my mouth reversing off his fingers. "We have to go," I said. It happened so subtly and quickly my kids hadn't even noticed. We ran to our nearby car, buckled in, and drove home. I spent the rest of the day in a windowless room in my basement shaking. It wasn't until the next day at the urging of a co-worker that I called police.

Why didn't I run? Scream? Kick? Slap? Report it immediately? Partly shock, perhaps, but I think I also didn't want to create a scene. Or perhaps I just froze, a common response to panic. Or maybe I wanted to be polite. I was definitely confused about what was happening and the implications.

In the crystalline clarity of hindsight I knew I'd been assaulted. I could have been strangled in broad daylight while my children watched. I'd wanted to model cooperation, and had imagined myself saying later, "Wasn't that nice man helpful?" But instead I modeled recklessness. My children were oblivious to my fear or its after-effects but they also didn't see me assert myself. I missed what is sometimes called a teachable moment on that paradoxical topic referred to as stranger-danger. We tell kids (especially girls) to be kind to others but also not to trust anyone they don't know well. This line is difficult to navigate, even for adults.

When you read about women who are assaulted physically or sexually you may wonder why they don't report it; I do. Beyond the many reasons offered — the fear of not being believed, of being slut-shamed or humiliated, of protracted legal battles that overwhelmingly don't yield convictions, or of suffering career repercussions — may I add one more? Women are raised to be gracious and polite, and to suck up a lot of discomfort. Most women are assaulted by men they know and often by men more powerful than they. Manners, it's been drilled into us, are a good thing. Except when they victimize us.

I saw my assailant again the next week near Toronto's Yonge and St. Clair Streets. This time, despite feeling panicky, I immediately whipped out my phone and called 9-1-1. I trailed him south toward Summerhill Avenue but he slipped out of my sight before the police arrived. Just that glimpse of the bearded man and I was breathless and sweaty; my heart raced.

My story is in no way unique. If anything positive comes out of my own experience, and a culture that's hopefully becoming more inclined to believe the assailants, I hope it's that we start to use our voices to protest more loudly, and support one another more proactively.

I know I will.

Alison DeLory is a writer, editor, publisher, teacher and consultant in Halifax. She is the author of two children's chapter books, Lunar Lifter (2012) and Scotia Sinker (2015) and has contributed to several anthologies. She has written news, feature stories and essays for publications including The Globe and Mail, Chatelaine, Today's Parent, Ryerson Magazine, Dalhousie Magazine, The Medical Post, Halifax Magazine, and Canadian Traveler. Alison teaches part-time at Mount Saint Vincent University in communication studies. For a full bio see www.alisondelory.com.

(Rishikesh, India)

Re - Connecting . . .

By Carrie Ellen Brummer (Muscat, Oman)

I **thought I'd come to India for a yoga festival.**

When I left Muscat for Rishikesh I decided to have no internet for the duration of the trip. I wanted to take in the sights, to paint, to practice yoga, and to make meaningful connections with the people I met.

I run a company from the internet. I was nervous: What if a client needed help? What if my website went down? What if someone tried to reach out and I wasn't there to respond?

I knew I needed a break. The constant compulsion to respond to every little notification sputtered out by my phone was wearing me down. I felt the anxiety of not being up to date on email, my messages with loved ones, you name it.

In the Moment — Real Life Stories of Hope and Inspiration

We took a cab to Rishikesh from the airport. I was inundated with visuals and noise. Cars honking. Motorbikes dodging cows standing in the street. People walking in bright colored saris. I got my camera out and breathed it all in. I looked over to someone next to me to share in the moment. They were on the phone.

I'd never traveled to India before and too many friends and loved ones had stories of "Delhi belly," or of the horror of such visible poverty. I can be such a worrier. I wondered, would I relax at all on this holiday? Yet, as I watched towns pass us as we tumbled down the dirt roads towards the ashram, I felt this wave of peace. I had no where I needed to be. No one expected anything of me. There was beauty in the dirt, color and noise around me. I felt strangely at home.

When we arrived at the ashram (a Hindu monastery) I sat quietly, taking in all of this new scenery. Loads of yogis fiddled on their phones telling loved ones they'd arrived, or uploading their first photo to Instagram. It felt weird not to have my phone out too.

Hindu gods lined the walkways where people came to pray, or show reverence to Lord Shiva by touching his statue's foot. Street dogs wandered past looking for food scraps. I could hear car horns blaring in the distance. I was brought back to my seat in the ashram when I heard someone ask, "Where is the internet?"

Once we settled into our rooms we walked into town to find dinner and explore the shops lining the street with scarves, kaftans and genie pants. We sat down at a table with immediate, waterside view of Mother Ganga, what many in the west call the River Ganges. I closed my eyes and took a deep breath. The sun's setting reflection flickered on the water. I wondered if I had time to do a small painting while we were there. We all smiled, sitting in peace and relaxation, happy to finally arrive in Rishikesh.

I heard someone in the restaurant ask, "What is the internet password?"

I began to wonder, will I survive without internet? It's everywhere I go! Should I quickly check my Facebook group to see how they are all doing? The funny thing was I expected the temptation to be strong. It wasn't. I knew I made a choice to disconnect and I was holding to it. That decision in itself was freeing.

There would be many more temptations to "connect" during my ten days in Rishikesh.

Each night there was an aarti, a ceremony with fire or light to pray and offer focused intention for someone or something. One particular night focused on letting go. We sat snuggled together in the cooling night air, listening to the crackle of the bonfire as the heat tickled our faces. We were given a betel nut and paper to write down something we wished to release. I sat staring at my piece of paper. What to let go?

We waited our turn then stood up to throw our paper and the nut into the fire, a symbolic release from the intention on that paper. I stared at my paper as flames engulfed it, charring it to black.

I thought of home and my constant need to be busy, always working on something new for the business or answering email. It all felt so distant, like I was on another planet. The tension so often present in my shoulders was noticeably absent. There was nowhere I should be or had to be. I was exactly where I needed to be. When I left the internet with my home back in Muscat, I wasn't just disconnecting from the celebration of busy in the world around me, it was an active choice to reconnect with me.

I really felt it on a night several of us went to dinner outside the ashram. We had ordered our meals and were waiting for the freshly cooked food, sometimes the waits could be quite a while. When I looked up from handing over the menu I glanced around me. Every single friend that joined me had their phone out, their screens casting a glow on their face in the dimly lit eating area. My heart sank. Here we were, sitting next to each other, "connected" but disconnected. How many moments have I missed in my life because my face is in a phone?

We walked to the orphanage through a tunnel of streets and worn down cement walls. I passed a woman sweeping dirt off her doorstep. The family cow moo-ed, while a dog and monkey fought over their corner of the street. The road was pebbled, made of dirt and uneven. Occasionally we'd see children's handprints painted on walls or on stones in the ground. That was our trail to follow. Out of the blue we walked into a little garden hideaway with woven chairs and tables. Green plants filled the spaces around the eating space and beautiful little painted signs said, "welcome."

A young man popped up out of nowhere as we admired the space.

"Hello," he said. "My name is Oinak. How many of you are there? I will help you today no problem."

Oinak led us to a little bamboo open garden area. Cushions on a rock bench and woven chairs surrounded a circular table. Babbling away, we chatted like the monkeys we passed on the streets. Some of the girls had their cell phones out as we looked through the menu. Oinak patiently waited as we chittered like a bunch of birds, asking questions about the menu and the orphanage. There was some teasing, too. Once our orders were collected we asked him to come back and talk to us more. He said, "I'll be back, I'll tell you my story." I didn't notice any cell phones out after that.

"I was born here." Oinak sat with us, his back tall. "I was born here in the orphanage."

All nine of us grew silent. We sat with this young man and hung onto his every word. We listened to the story of the orphanage, founded by a western woman who found her calling sitting alongside Mother Ganga. He talked about how despite having little funds she has built an orphanage and school. The orphanage houses 60 children and more than 200 students go to school there every day. If their parents make less than 1 dollar a day, they qualify to attend the orphanage school.

Oinak talked about how they all help out. Everyone helps in their own way. Some cook and serve food in the very cafe we were sitting in. Other's helped harvest food or the cow's milk from their dairy cows. You wouldn't know of the obstacles he faced from his relaxed posture. His smile was from ear to ear as we asked questions and listened. Oinak was articulate and conveyed a maturity I've observed in few 18 year olds.

"I'm so grateful," he said. "I have so much because of this place. And now I'm going to school to become a lawyer."

He beamed as he talked of his aspirations. I looked down, feeling so full of emotion hearing this. We all sat in silent, tearful appreciation. And gratitude.

Thank you Oinak.

Carrie Brummer is an artist and educator who believes engaging with our creative interests makes us happier, healthier, more fulfilled human beings. She created her community www.ArtistStrong.com to help everyone honor their desire to be creative. Our world is better for your creativity.

Cultivate your creativity today by joining her free art exploration series www.SoulBrushSessions.com.

(One of two bridges in Rishikesh crossing the River Ganges)

(Our Hindu monastery)

Finding the Best in People at their Worst

By Ian Lawton (Sydney, Australia)

They say to love your enemies, but no one tells you how to do it. It's easy to think nice thoughts about difficult people when you're alone, but how do you love the annoying work colleague, you know the one who's like a shiver looking for a spine to run up. We're supposed to find the best in people, but how do you do it? How do find the best in a person that even tele-marketers hang up on?

Sometimes you can remove difficult people from your life, and sometimes that's exactly the right thing to do, BUT, on the other hand...

Sometimes you can't. Sometimes they're your boss in a job you need. Sometimes they're a brother-in-law and you don't want to lose touch with your sister. Some-times they're an ex and you need to co parent. Sometimes they move in next door. Sometimes they're on the other end of an important service call. You get the point.

And in any case, can't we do better than create a cocoon of people we like? As Socrates said in Peaceful Warrior, "Those who are hardest to love need it the most." They need it. WE need it. It makes us better people to stretch beyond the safety of people who ignite us.

Think of it this way. Every act of love brings light to the world. If loving your family and friends lights up a room, imagine how far reaching the light, deep within and out to the corners of the earth, when you break through the shell of familiarity and love a stranger or beat down a wall and love someone you dislike.

The world desperately needs the sort of love that stretches to the moon and back and collects all the strays, monsters, foes and nemeses on its way. The question remains-yes, but how do you find the beauty in the beast?

Let's get practical here. How do you see the best in people acting their worst?

EVERY person has some redeeming qualities. I mean everyone, by virtue of being alive, has some goodness in them. This includes global terrorists, Vladimir Putin, Lance Armstrong, the sunshine club at Westboro Baptist Church and yes it even includes politicians. My philosophy is that everyone is basically good but really, really scared. Hence the many strange choices WE make.

Mother Theresa said, "Everybody has something good inside them. Some hide it, some neglect it, but it is there."

Take as an example the movie, Gran Torino, with Clint Eastwood playing the most hate filled character imaginable. And yet we love him. We root for him. We love him because we want to find something redeeming in his character. He treats his Asian neighbors so badly and yet they see it. After he saves the teenage boy next door from a local gang, the boy's sister says to him, "You're a better man to him than our own father was. You're a good man." What is this goodness she sees?

Maybe it's his HONESTY. He speaks his mind without a filter. Some of the people we find difficult have no filters. They say things the rest of us think in the privacy of our own minds. They offend us. They shock us. They scare us with their jaded perspective on life, even though we know they have a half truth. They are honest, and honesty is one of THE most virtuous qualities.

Maybe it's his DETERMINATION. He has values and won't back down. Some of the people we find difficult frustrate us with what we see as stubbornness. And yet we could learn a thing or two from their deter-mination.

Maybe it's his CREATIVITY. Cranky people amaze me with their creative wit. The repartee between Eastwood and his Italian barber is priceless. They verbally spar without missing a beat. We don't have to abuse each other. But we can learn from the creativity of cranks.

Maybe it's his RESILIENCE. He's a hard man for a reason. He's seen a few things and learnt how to protect himself. That shows incredible resilience. We don't have to harden ourselves or close the world out, but we can learn from the resilience of the battle weary.

Without too much thought, I've come up with four qualities that we might admire in a difficult person. There are so many more. And this is just the beginning point. Find something, anything, redeeming in the diffi-cult person, and you will be on the path to respecting them, or at least tolerating them.

As I grow older, I find that raw honesty inspires me more than anything; people who have been touched by the harshest parts of life and its left them real, worldly wise, even a little hard headed, brave, worn out but still trying, shaken but not stirred. Unpre-tentious, battle scarred, prone to shock you by saying the things you're thinking, willing to see things most people turn away from, cranky honesty is disarming but beautiful in its own way.

Now switch gears. So far, it's all been about the other person. Let me let you in on a little secret. I could populate a small city with people who find me difficult. The lesson here is really for me, and what I can learn about myself. Life is a school and diffi-cult people are the faculty. Difficult inter-actions are the class. So don't avoid them or you will never graduate into the fullest version of who you can be.

Difficult is SO subjective. We find people difficult because they hold up a mirror and we don't like everything we see. Learn to love your own cranky qualities, and you will have less resistance and conflict with cranks and monsters around you.

And maybe the most important lesson

(Clint Eastwood in Gran Torino)

of all from Gran Torino is that people are complex, they have all sorts of conflicting motives and experiences. And they change! Eastwood is protecting his worldview, his community, at least what he thinks is best for his neighborhood. He thinks his Asian neighbors are the problem, only to later find that he needs to protect them to safeguard a culture he values. He changed. People change. We ALL change. Be slow to judge.

Oscar Wilde said it well, "Everyone may not be good, but there's always something good in everyone. Never judge anyone because every saint has a past and every sinner has a future."

Compiled by Gary Doi

Ian Lawton (soulseeds.com) is a spiritual leader of a growing world-wide community with a 20 year background in pastoral, change and grief support. He is an author and lectures internationally on contemporary spirituality. He has been blogging and writing daily affirmations for several years. Ian and his wife Meg are the founders of Soulseeds – a site designed to help make people's lives and this world a thriving garden.

The Beauty of Old Friendships

By Tara Rummell Berson (Middletown, New Jersey)

In the Moment — *Real Life Stories of Hope and Inspiration*

"The best mirror is an old friend." ~
Peter Nivio Zarlenga, Author

There's something truly priceless about the friends who have known you for what feels like an eternity – your "old" friends. They're the ones who didn't come into your life for a reason or a season, but the kind of relationships that have flourished over the years and will continue to thrive until your last breath. Like a song from your past playing on the radio, old friendships can transport you to good times in your life that bring a genuine smile to your face and warm your heart.

Think back to some of the early healthy friendships you formed. While growing up, these friends became a home base you could return to – your safety net, your defender, your shoulder to cry on, and your source of humor. Flash forward to the present: If you've been lucky enough to hold on to these relationships over the years – the people you've belly laughed with, shared dreams, disappointments and dilemmas with, took adventures with, and now looking back, celebrated all of your major life events with – you are blessed with the gift of friendship.

I was reminded of this special gift when one of my college girlfriends got married last year. Finding time to see your friends can be ridiculously hard to coordinate between work, vacation and kids' schedules, which is why I was so grateful that she did our tight-knit group a favor by deciding to get hitched! It's amazing how a happy and momentous occasion can easily bring a band back together. It's a "life moment," and that's something that old friends really don't like to miss out on.

We're all in our early forties now, but when I'm with these girls it's easy to feel 20 again. We all pledged the same sorority together back in the spring of 1993, and it's so comforting and refreshing to be with these women. I think you feel most like yourself when you're around people who have known you for a long time. I guess that's because old friends remind you of a time when it was just you. A time before you had a career, a spouse, kids, or life's pressures to really worry about. It was just you – and them. Your chosen pack to walk through life with.

After we were fortunate enough to spend a chunk of quality time together, one of the girls said, "My face hurts from laughing. Being with you all is good for my soul."

I couldn't agree more. Between the hilarious stories we were recounting from our college days (when we were a bit more reckless and uninhibited), the old school dance moves we were busting out together on the dance floor (remember the Roger Rabbit and the Running Man?!), and the warm feeling that was flowing through our veins knowing that we really "get" (and still accept!) each other, is truly a bond that can never be broken.

I never had a sister, but these girls have felt like sisters to me. We've held each other's hands during hardships and heartache, celebrated in each other's accomplishments, and have always "shown up" whenever and wherever we were needed. Regardless of how near or far we live, or whatever life phase we're going through, these friendships have remained a stable and constant force.

Friendships like this have been cultivated over decades. The opening quote by author Peter Nivio Zarlenga ("The best mirror is an old friend.") is true. An old

(Celebrating our friend's wedding, 2015)

friend is an honest reflection of your past as well as your reality. Looking into their eyes can help you see yourself more clearly, and often no words even need to be exchanged. Their knowledge of your history, personality and patterns can help you gain perspective and fit together the pieces of your life puzzle.

When you make these friendships as adolescents, there's no way that you could even fathom all of life's ups and downs that you're going to ride through together: job pressures, marital issues, health scares, the agony of not being able to have a child, the death of a loved one…

Our life's journey may be unpredictable, but these steadfast and unfailing friendships can help you manage the uncertainty.

We can't imagine what the future holds for each of us, but we can cherish the people who have been there to help us navigate through life. These beautiful friendships will continue to provide the wind when your sail is stuck, the hope when you don't have any, the laughter when you really, really need it. While you may not be able to see or speak to these friends on a daily basis, their hearts are with you every day so you are never alone.

Tara Rummell Berson is a writer, editor and blogger. She's been on staff at REDBOOK magazine and has contributed to numerous national media outlets. In 2011, she launched The Crankiness Crusher ™, an online platform that encourages people to focus on the big and small things that bring them happiness on a daily basis. She lives a blissfully chaotic life at the Jersey Shore with her husband, two elementary school-aged children, two dogs and a fish.

PHOTOGRAPHIC MOMENT
Linden Maniquet at Darren & Domenica's Wedding
Photo Credit: Gary Doi

Above:

WATER TAXI RIDE
Xincheng Ancient Water Town
Photo credit, Francisco Little

Making Sense

By Laura Best (East Dalhousie, Nova Scotia)

The sudden passing of a friend in February kind of threw me for a loop. For a few days I withdrew into my thoughts to contemplate the things I would miss with this friend no longer here, and to honour the memories I had of her. Whenever we lose someone in our life it causes us to reflect upon so many things—the frailty of life being one of them, our own mortality as well as the mortality of those closest to us, the things we haven't yet accomplished that we'd like to, the relationships we forge and so, so much more.

When we get to a certain age, we begin to understand that life doesn't always make sense. Good things happen, bad things happen, and we have no idea why. We can become angry and bitter over the things we deem senseless in this world and yet delight when good things happen that also don't make sense. (If that makes sense!)

I'm not sure that life is supposed to make sense. If it did make sense all the time, I think we'd lose a little of the wonder and the magic that exists in the world. And without the wonder and the magic what would that do to our hopes and dreams and wishes? Without magic I'm almost certain all those things wouldn't exist. Why would we ever wish for something or allow our hopes to propel us into some crazy new direction, why would set our dreams on anything other than the reality we now have if there wasn't some force out there capable of making our hopes, dreams and wishes come true? Wouldn't we simply go through our days and wait for life to happen? How drab, how utterly mundane and ordinary, how sad.

Truthfully, I'm glad to live in a world that doesn't always make sense, where strange, out of the ordinary things sometimes happen, where people overcome insurmountable odds, a world that fills us with delight and yes, sometimes, sorrow. My friend once sent me a link to a site about fairy homes. There are those who might say that a site like that doesn't make any sense, and maybe it doesn't, but so what?

If I was looking for things to always make sense I might have said a long time ago there's no sense in trying to get published. I might have said it's too hard of a thing to accomplish. I might have looked at the stats from some of the literary magazines I submitted to (we receive over 1200 submissions a year and publish 5%) and said the odds are not in my favour. I might have said, I have no one to show me the way. I might have counted the rejections (I had a few file folders filled) and said it isn't meant to be. I might have said I've never once taken a writing course. I might have said I don't know one single solitary writer in the entire world. But I didn't say those things. I kept doing what I was doing even though there were times that it didn't make sense to be doing it. (Seriously, some of my friends worried about the postage I was spending and if it was actually "paying off") I kept wishing and hoping and dreaming…and writing.

And for those people who think life makes perfect sense, that if we dig deep enough we'll find out exactly why things happen, I feel a little sad. I might be a Pollyanna, I might set my sights on things that seem an impossibility, but I'd rather live in a world of magic and wonder than a world that just is.

R.I.P my friend–the next time I find a fairy house in the woods I'll think of you.

Laura Best (lauraabest.wordpress. com) has had over forty short stories published in literary magazines and anthologies. Her first young adult novel, "Bitter, Sweet," was short listed for the Geoffrey Bilson Award for Historical Fiction for Young People and made the Best Books for Kids and Teens 2011 list. Her second novel is "Flying With A Broken Wing".

An Inch of Water

Poem & Artwork by Leslie Silton
(Los Angeles, California)

when I am hanging from the ledge
feet growing heavy
hands and fingers weary
slippery with sweat

the long free-fall flight seems safe and soothing
I will fall downward
Sometimes
I dream I am a bird on wing
catching updrafts instead

I am a feather-covered human kite
sailing into the sun
my trajectory curving with the earth

when I am hanging from the ledge
I forget
who made that ledge
who wanted that ledge to be there

when I am hanging from the ledge
I feel I can only dream of firm ground.
That place -- like faith --
that only exists
once one decides it is there

Firm ground:
I had forgotten
how a person can nearly drown in an inch of water.
All I have to do,
all I ever had to do
to be saved
was simply
stand up

Leslie Silton (leslie.silton@prodigy.net) began her artistic career as a poet in 1965. Over the years her poems have been reprinted in various small press and online websites. She has participated in over 150 open readings. 2006 turned her passion for writing into a day job, freelancing as a book editor and writing coach. Three of her short stories can be found on the web and her modern-day sci-fi novel "The Gift Horse" is available on Amazon.com.

A Letter to my Daughter

By Zee Gorman (San Francisco, California)

(As part of a Psychology Class assignment, my daughter needed a letter from me. This is what I wrote.)

I still can't believe I am so lucky: I brought a little girl to this world as I had fantasized when I was a little girl myself. Well, your daddy helped a little bit.

I still remember the day when I was lying in the doctor's office confirming my pregnancy. For the first time, I heard your heartbeats: So fast, so strong, and so steady. My tears of joy rolled down my cheeks. It was the kind of joy I had never experienced before. It was unbelievable.

Things have only gotten better after that day.

On Christmas 1996, I received the test result of my ultrasound: You were to be a healthy baby! It was the best Christmas present I had ever gotten my whole life! I thanked the nurse who called me and gave me this news, over and over again.

You came out a week before your due day, looking chubby and smooth like a one-year-old. It was hard to believe that you were in my tummy only hours ago. That night, after the nurse bathed you and wrapped you in a soft blanket, they placed you next to my chest. I listened to your breathing. So calm. So sweet. I felt like I lived in a fantasy world where everything was magical.

Eighteen years. It has been so much joy watching you grow from a little girl into a young woman with your own personality and characteristics. There have been too many remarkable and memorable moments to count: The first time I let you walk to your classroom from the curbside; the first time I let you walk to school by yourself; and the first time I let you drive to the mall by yourself. . . . We've had so many first times together; we still have so many to look forward to.

(Zee and her toddler daughter)

(Continued on the next page)

Compiled by Gary Doi

I'm sorry but I just have to be sappy for a moment as a mother. To have a child at all is a wonder; and to have a child like you, beautiful, healthy, independent, self-aware, sensitive, kind, smart, and sweet, . . . is simply heaven itself.

There are many things I want to share with you. Most of them have to do with what I have learned in my life that was surprising. Perhaps counter-intuitive in a way. As you are dealing with life's various challenges, perhaps these lessons might help.

1. Others do not read your mind. Daddy taught me this. This is a man who would do anything for me and yet, despite the fact that we are so close, he would not know when I appreciate a bit of quietness, when I crave for a Chinese feast, and when I get homesick. If I don't say anything, he would think that I want to be talked to, that I want hamburger for dinner, and I'm happy to be out exploring the countryside. The truth is: Everyone is different so nobody can predict what your personal needs are at any specific moment. I'm so glad Daddy and I learned this lesson together, which is the fundamental reason why we have such a happy marriage. So what I want you to take away is: Never feel bad for what you want and always make it clear to those who can provide it. Know that if they love you, they would be more than happy to provide it to you.

2. Sometimes you have to do your best and not ask for anything in return. There will be times when you feel you are at a dead end. Nothing you do seems to be changing the result. In those times, you simply have to keep at it, because life has a way to surprise you. You don't want to give up before the pleasant surprise comes, because then you will miss it. Learn to cope. This is one of the most important lessons of life.

3. You always have a choice. Even when it doesn't appear to be so. You have the choice to let others bully you, or you can fight back; you have the choice to put yourself down, or you can learn the lesson and move on; you have the choice to blame yourself, or you can forgive yourself; you have the choice to accept who you are or you can transform yourself; you can choose to live up to others' dreams or be happy with your own. The possibilities in life are unlimited. Know yourself. That's the first step. Accept yourself—the second. And transform yourself to the beauty you admire—that's in your own choice too.

Sweetie—Life has only just started. The road ahead is full of adventure. All you have to bring with you is yourself: your natural wits and smartness, your passion, your wants, and your bag of tricks. Be patient with yourself and be patient with life. Stay open and positive to all possibilities. Be kind. Be courageous. Be generous. Find your true potential.

You will be a wonderful person. I can't wait to walk the coming years with you and enjoy every moment together.

Love,
Mom

(Zee and her teenage daughter, 2015)

Zee Gorman (zeegorman.blogspot.ca): Born in South China during the Cultural Revolution, Zee was raised within layers of political and cultural confines. Yet her love for literature gave wings to her imagination of a life completely different from her destined path. She has written short stories, poems, and essays, and is mildly published in China. Her quest for a new life eventually led to her migration to the United States where she completed two Master's Degrees. Today, Zee Gorman lives in Northern California with her husband and her two daughters. By night she is a writer and an artist, and by day she has a career in IT management.

Moments That Matter

"Sometimes the moments that challenge us the
most, define us."   - Deena Kastor

"Lone Bull"— Roy Henry Vickers

Our lives changed forever that day – December 11, 1961.

My older sister Shirley and I were walking home from our elementary school which was located close to our reserve in Nanaimo, BC. As always, we came straight home after class. Dad didn't allow any after school events or activities, not even a visit to a friend's house.

We were only a few hundred yards away from our reserve when a blue car stopped in front of us. Two serious-looking women stepped out and told us to get in the car. We didn't know what to do. We were only six and eight years old. They were the grown-ups, so we obeyed. Thus began the most terrifying experience of my life, one that haunts me to this day.

The strangers drove us to the Social Services office and there we sat for what seemed like hours. We were frightened and confused. When someone brought our younger sister Josephine into the room, we cried and pleaded to be taken home. One of the social workers promised we would soon see our dad.

The truth was we would never be with our dad—ever again.

Instead, we were taken to a foster home run by two retired preachers. The foster parents had four kids of their own and six First Nations children. We were treated much differently than the preachers' children.

It was a sad and lonely time. We longed for our family on the reserve. The foster parents 'taught us' to disown our language and culture, saying it was dirty and shameful. We were severely punished if caught speaking our native language. We were tortured and beaten for the smallest infractions such as making eye contact with the other First Nations children. The foster mom would grab us by our hair or use a leather belt to hit us across the back or the arm.

It particularly distressed me when the foster mom hurt my sisters. Even though I was normally shy and withdrawn, I would stand there and stare at her. I watched in absolute silence, defying her to stop. When she did, she directed her anger at me.

"Take that look off your face!" she'd scream. She'd slap me until she felt my 'look' was gone. Then I was locked in my bedroom as 'attitude and bad behaviour' were not tolerated.

"You have such round cheeks," Shirley would tease, "because Foster Mom hit you so many times."

We laughed about that. The truth was we all tried to look out for one another.

The rules of the foster home allowed parents to visit once a year. Seeing our father was bittersweet. Of course, we were thrilled to see Dad but the time with him was brief. All too soon, he'd be gone.

One day when I was twelve, we received a call that Dad would not be coming to visit anymore. He had passed away. Our family on the reserve wanted us girls to attend the

Healing

By Roberta Price (Richmond, BC)

"Forgiveness is fundamental to healing"
– Roberta Price

funeral but the foster parents refused.

"If you go on reserve, they will keep you," they warned. "They are bad people."

We were heart-broken and angry.

Our home environment was terrifying and disturbing – not just for us – but for all of the foster children. In fact, to get away from the beatings, three of the other First Nations teenagers ran away from the home and headed to the streets. Many years later I learned that they all died at a young age: one committed suicide at age 29, one died the day he turned 31 from HIV and another was murdered.

When Shirley was eighteen years old she left the home. She had met someone and they were married soon after. I ran away when I was in grade twelve to live with Shirley. I felt bad leaving Josephine behind.

Years later I began to realize how much was taken from us. Instead of being raised in a supportive home environment, we were subjected to a steady diet of ridicule, discrimination and abuse. We were made to feel unworthy and shameful of our past. We had no self-esteem; we had no foundation to build a life and a future. We had lost our identity as the language and traditions of the 'larger society' were driven into us. We no longer saw ourselves as children of the Coast Salish. We were forced to become different people.

It was the Elders who helped me understand that truth, which turned my life around. They taught me, cared for me, prayed for me and most of all, loved me. I am eternally grateful to them for their guidance and wisdom. They re-connected me to my roots, and told me my family history.

I was born Priscilla Roberta Bob. On my father's side, I am Coast Salish from Snuneymuxw, (Nanaimo) First Nation meaning "the Great Peoples". I am the granddaughter of Jonah and Mariah Bob and Ben and Anastasia Canute. On my mother's side, I am Coast Salish from the Cowichan, "the land warmed by the sun".

My father, Robert Bob Senior, was a fisherman in charge of the shellfish beds in his community. Before that, he had been a longshoreman, logger and a miner. My parents married through an arranged agreement, an exchange of goods between the Bob family and the Canute family. This was the second marriage for each of my parents.

The marriage, however, did not go well. Mother was unhappy, not necessarily with my father, but with his family. She felt that Dad's family did not accept her. After many years of struggle and frustration, Mother requested permission of great grandmother Josephine Canute to end the marriage and go home. By the time she finally agreed, my parents had a family of four children: Kelly (age 6), Shirley (age 4), Roberta (age 2) and Josephine (newborn). Grandmother Mariah Bob insisted the children stay in Snuneymuxw (Nanaimo).

After Mother left the family, Father did his best to care for us. When he was away fishing, my grandmother, grandfather, and siblings from Dad's first marriage looked after us.

Grandmother encouraged Dad to get his education and to read and speak both English and our native language. As a result, he learned to write and speak fluently in both languages and was well read. One of my fondest memories is Dad telling stories and reading to us when we went to bed. But, because of my 'abduction' in 1961, I have very few memories of my dad.

Our story was not an isolated one. The practice of removing First Nations children from their families and communities had been going on for generations. Decades of racist government policies conspired against First Nations people and robbed them of their children, culture and their dignity and

(Left to right: Josephine, Me, Dad & Shirley, 1960)

(My brother Kelly)

Lower Mainland helping disenfranchised aboriginals to love and learn their traditional ways. My great-aunties taught my brother about our cultural practices and beliefs. Now he is a well respected Elder married into the Squamish Nation. Eugene was the only one of my mother's twelve children that retained his language despite the various attempts to 'take the Indian out of the child' at Kuper Island Residential School.

The actions against Aboriginal people in Canada spanned many generations and it will take many generations to heal. Some individuals may never heal. Others died long before our people even knew there was a possibility of reconciliation. Reconciliation is a turning point for healing our children, grandchildren and great grandchildren who have suffered greatly.

For me, one of the important steps in healing is to be able to forgive those who hurt me, my family and all Aboriginal people. Forgiveness is an action as well as a feeling. Even if you say "I forgive", you may not feel forgiveness for a long time.

But, eventually it does come and you feel free and at peace with yourself.

Today, I am a mother of four children and eight grandchildren. I am no longer the shy, withdrawn girl of my youth but a woman who speaks for those who do not have a voice. I am proud of my heritage and proud to be an Elder in my culture, teaching others our traditional ways.

It is my passion and I am making a difference in people's lives.

well-being. It first happened through the residential schools, and then, through the child protection system, as in the case of Shirley, Josephine and me.

Our family also experienced the residential schools. Years before our abduction, the authorities came and took my brother Kelly (at age three), to the notorious Kuper Island Residential School in the Southern Gulf Islands. Kelly stayed there until he was eighteen. He died at the age of twenty-four.

My mom's third child Eugene Harry (from her first marriage) was also taken to Kuper Island. The first time the police came, my mother's aunt and uncle hid Eugene in a potato sack. The police walked around the outside, beating the bushes to scare the children out. My brother said he felt he would die.

Eugene Harry now works in Vancouver's Downtown Eastside and other places in the

Roberta Price has been and continues to be a voice of courage, hope and strength for aboriginal people on the road to recovery. With gratitude and respect to the many people who have helped and loved her along the way, Roberta has developed the power and depth of her healing strength as an Elder.

Roberta has been employed by many community and provincial organizations in British Columbia, sitting on Boards, working in many schools and helping individuals with their life journey. For example, she has participated as an Elder with: UBC's Learning Exchange (a community engagement initiative based in Vancouver's Downtown Eastside); School District 37, Delta; School District 38, Richmond; School District 41, Burnaby (Aboriginal Enhancement Agreement Committee); Aboriginal Wellness Health Centre with Vancouver Coastal Health ("Awaken the Inner Healer"); Vancouver Native Health (Indigenous Elders Partnership Program); UBC School of Nursing; and Native Education Centre, Vancouver (Instructor).

FACE TO FACE

By Marion Iberg (Langley, BC)

"The white building…see, at the top of the hill? That's the Area Development Project office—the ADP office," Enrique, our World Vision Peru escort says in broken English.

In the Moment — Real Life Stories of Hope and Inspiration

"Yes," I answer, trembling with excitement. In a few minutes I will meet Jhomara, my fifteen-year-old sponsored child. I feel in awe of the event that's about to happen. Not every sponsor has the opportunity for such a special visit.

At nine o'clock sharp, Enrique met my friend and me at our hotel in Lima. During the hour and ten minute taxi ride to Ventanilla, he answered our questions and provided information to help us understand the area

where my child lives. Enrique's passion and dedication for his work with World Vision is impressive. He is proud of his English and often checks to see if we understand.

As we near our destination, I show him the last thank you letter from my child and the photo of her standing beside a chair displaying articles I had sent for Christmas.

"She is in sports," he says.

"Yes. How do you know?"

"She is wearing her sports uniform. School children have two uniforms if they are in sports: one for regular class and one for sports."

Wow, I just learned something. How different from my culture, where track suits are sometimes worn as casual wear.

Our taxi driver turns off the pavement onto a dusty road, avoiding dogs, pedestrians and bikes. Past open doors, gaping eyes and broken fences crowding the edges of the dirt street, we chug up the bumpy hill. Higher and higher we drive until we turn abruptly into the ADP yard.

The driver manoeuvers around a huge water tank. As he backs up, I see the tops of mottled tin roofs beneath us. Stop, for Heaven's sake. Where are the abutments? I close my eyes. The driver stops on the edge of a sheer drop-off to the valley below.

I get out and look down on patched tin and board roofs. Farther away, tiny shacks pepper the desert valley and opposite hillside. Never have I seen such poverty. Until today, I wondered if World Vision embellished photos of children in poverty-stricken communities to generate more sponsorships and donations. I now know first-hand, they do not. I begin to understand why in every letter, Jhomara thanks me for sponsoring her.

After introductions, Ronald, the Coordinator of ADP Ventanilla, and Erika, his assistant, take us into the centre of the building and lead us up two flights of narrow

stairs open to the elements.

"We never see much sun this time of year," Enrique says. "October is always cloudy fog."

I hardly hear his words. My heart is pounding.

We are ushered into a meeting room containing a large table and several chairs. I am struck by the simplicity and the meager surroundings. No fancy computers or office furniture here. I'm surprised, but pleased. All the more money for children and programs.

My attention turns to the World Vision representatives chattering in Spanish. I can tell they are looking for Jhomara.

Enrique translates, "She was here. Where did she go?"

I struggle to breathe as fear constricts my throat. Did she leave? We arrived only ten minutes late.

Seconds later, Jhomara bolts through the door into my arms. Although she is shorter than I envisioned from the pictures, I recognize her instantly. I clutch my World Vision child and feel her tight embrace. We stand heart to heart, soul to soul. There is an immediate connection. Warmth swirls through me. I blink back tears of joy.

We break the hug and hold each other at arm's length, looking into one another's faces. She is beaming. I can't stop smiling.

"I love you," she says in English.

What a gift this child is, so open and warm. I am humbled, realizing my sponsorship is an honour.

We sit down, oblivious to others seated around the table watching us. Through the translator, Jhomara asks about my health, family and travels. She gives me a letter and picture she created for this occasion and studies my face as Enrique translates. The words and artwork make me blink and swallow.

I hand her a pretty bag. "I brought you

(Posing with Jhomara, my fifteen-year-old sponsored child)

In the Moment — Real Life Stories of Hope and Inspiration

gifts."

Jhomara politely goes through the presents until she discovers the red hoodie. She promptly puts it on and runs her fingers over the raised letters.

"Canada," she says, smiling. "Gracias."

I draw her attention to the miniature silver angel hanging from the zipper. She zips up the hoodie and fingers the tiny angel. Her eyes sparkle as she grins. I give gifts to her for family and pens and pencils to share at school.

We are offered a treat, Turron de Doña Pepa, a type of cake traditionally served in October. How appropriate, it is October 6th. Eating, we watch a video in Spanish of the community programs and listen while the staff speaks of the Ventanilla project successes. Jhomara loses interest and instead admires the red jacket she wears, stroking the arms and caressing the letters.

After the video and talk, five of us head to the waiting taxi. Enrique sits in the front. Jhomara, Erika, my friend and I cram onto the tiny back seat. I hardly notice the bumpy ride as the taxi heads down the hill… or the cramped quarters. I feel as if I'm in a dream. After years of separation by country, continent and ocean, I sit close to my World Vision child. My heart overflows with joy. I crane my neck to look at her. Jhomara's smile is wide; her eyes, warm. She reaches for my hand.

The taxi stops in front of a World Vision library, one of thirteen library projects in the area. A Children's Supporter who runs the library is pleased to show us around. There are no more than fifty books on the book rack. My teacher eyes scan the room. Calendar corner, reading centre, painting easel, puppet centre, games, puzzles, colourful posters and children's art remind me of kindergarten classrooms back home. In stark contrast to the poverty beyond the walls, the library creates a safe place for young children to learn. I'm surrounded by happy faces, chatter, laughter and cooperation. A girl about twelve years of age, helps the younger children. I see evidence of her pride, confidence and high self-esteem.

"You will make a great teacher," I say to her.

She smiles as Enrique translates.

After the library tour, Jhomara and I sit at one of the small tables. From time to time we hold hands or embrace. Enrique comes over. "What message do you have for your sponsor?" he asks Jhomara in Spanish.

Jhomara looks at me. "Love your family. They are most important to you in the whole world."

Enrique translates and turns to me. "And your message to your sponsored child?"

"Work hard at school because education will help you live a life without poverty. You are beautiful. The stars smile upon you." My answer seems inadequate with the word love absent.

We take numerous photos and then our visit comes to an end. Once again we cram into the taxi. I decide to switch places with my friend. Only a few minutes remain of the visit with my World Vision child and I want to be near her.

As we speed along the pavement, Jhomara points to strings of shanties on the hillside.

"My community," she says in English.

I am appalled by the sight. From the look of the outsides of the shacks, I have no desire to view the insides.

A short time later, the taxi driver pulls off the highway. We say our goodbyes and Erika and Jhomara get out.

Enrique explains, "They will walk up the hill to the ADP office."

Our taxi circles around and pulls onto the highway. I look back, waving. Jhomara and Erika walk toward the dirt road. Still wearing the red hoodie, Jhomara waves at me with two hands as she walks. Then, with a broad grin she lifts the angel, touches it and blows a kiss my way.

I lose sight of Jhomara as we speed down the highway. Only later do I learn the reason for our quick retreat. In this impoverished area, theft is a way of life. Sometimes, a car transporting foreigners is ambushed and the tourists robbed.

On the journey back to the Lima hotel, I ride in a state of euphoria, amazed by the day's events and the magnitude of a dream fulfilled. Today, my World Vision Peruvian child and I met face to face.

The precious moments we spent together are now memories I will forever cherish.

Marion Iberg is a retired teacher with ten years' experience teaching elementary school students. In previous years, she was a partner in a dairy farm business where she was involved in all aspects of running the farm. Farm life, and personal and childhood experiences have created ideas for Marion's writings.

Story Teller

By Kathleen King-Hunt (Cowichan Valley, BC)

(Enjoying a book with my mother, 1965)

Ever the gifted story-teller, Mother wove her stories with charm and wit. "When I was born, my parents blessed me in the traditional Nuxalk beaver ceremony," she said pausing ever so slightly for effect. "That's why I am always busy."

"I am from Bella Coola on the BC Coast. The Nuxalk peoples say that Bella Coola means beautiful place—seriously beautiful. Sister mountains, rushing rivers and home to the thunderbird." Her words were organic and comforting. They flowed.

If the old adage that everyone has a book inside of them is true, then it was especially true of my mother. Her book may not have been packaged into nice, neat chapters because her life wasn't that way, but she always had something interesting to share—with anyone who cared to listen.

In my early teen years growing up in suburban Ontario, I remember going on errands with Mother. She'd chat with people wherever we went – the doctor's office or in the line-up at a local grocery store. She'd talk about her home, birthplace, family… anything about British Columbia or native people.

"Mom, how do you know so many people?" I asked her after one of our outings.

"Well, I didn't know those people before," she replied. "But I do now."

Mother always wanted to look her best and would braid her long strands of thick hair in the latest style. It was like she was dressing to be on centre stage. In the day where outfits matched, she updated her dresses and skirts using her old-fashioned sewing machine. To add a finishing touch, she'd select a piece of handmade native jewelry to wear. She was proud of her heritage, her parents and her native name Anuk'palslayc.

Mother conveyed her love and passion for live theatre to her family. During the fall and winter, we attended various shows and concerts. I still remember the award winning plays by Tomson Highway, a Cree artist. In the summer months, my mother took us with her as she followed the Pow Wow Circuit. At the competitions we enjoyed a wide range of native performers: singers, dancers, respected elders, songwriters and traditional teachers.

In the 1980s Mother's interest shifted to opera. Over time, with her guidance, I learned to enjoy the opera and the rich and gorgeous voices.

About that time, Mother's stories changed. They became more serious, often revealing the hardships of Canadian natives and the impact of government policies.

One evening my mother and I attended the performance of Puccini's opera Madame Butterfly at the old opera house in Toronto. We so looked forward to the show. As we waited for the opening scene, I expected Mom to talk about the libretto (the text) as she usually did, so I wouldn't get lost in the dramatic Italian songs. Instead, she asked a question.

"Do you know what enfranchisement means?"

I looked at her, my eyebrows furrowed. How did 'enfranchisement' fit with the opera?

Mother leant closer and lowered her voice. "Enfranchisement is a legal process for terminating a person's native status." She settled back and continued.

"My dream has always been to go to college," she said in a steady voice. "Now that all you kids are grown up and pursuing careers, I want to do the same. In order to go to college, I need to update my grade 8 to grade 12. But, there is a problem. My past has been erased. My childhood school records are not available. Not one school record." Tears welled up in Mom's eyes. She reached into her purse for a tissue.

Frowning, I turned to her. "What do you mean…your past is erased…your school records gone? How can that be?"

Mom explained that when she married Dad, a non-native, and moved from B.C. to Ontario, her previous status to the Nuxalk Nation was revoked or taken away somehow. Her maiden name had been completely removed from the records.

"Without identity records," she said, "it will be difficult to pursue my dream."

Mom's comments took me by surprise. I was shaken. Not knowing what to say, I just held my Mother's hand to comfort her. Then, the theatre lights dimmed and the audience grew quiet. The curtain rose as the symphony-sized orchestra began playing the lyric beauty of Puccini's score.

When I think about that moment today, I realize Mother's comments were less about being victimized and more about a declaration to overcome a challenge.

Soon after, she enrolled in an adult education school completion program. After several years of study, she received her grade 12 certificate at the age of fifty. Then, in 1985, the Federal government passed legislation (Bill C31) bringing the Indian Act in line with gender equality under the Canadian Charter of Rights and Freedoms. Mother's native status had been forcibly enfranchised due to discriminatory provisions. The new legislation meant that she was, once again, a proud member of the Nuxalk Nation.

There was no stopping Mother after that. She continued to enroll in various post-secondary programs to further her education. In addition to her interest in storytelling, Mother had a passion for writing. She completed the En'okwin Centre writing program in British Columbia. The program was exactly what she needed and wanted.

Now Mother was able to share stories

not only through the oral tradition of the Nuxalk Nation but also by writing stories about her home – the environment, eagles, butterflies, potlatches and mountains – and proudly sign her name as an author.

(My parents, Lena and Holly KIng, in a spoon canoe, 1959)

Kathleen King-Hunt is a proud member of the Nuxalk Nation. Currently, she resides and works on Coast Salish territory. In her role as District Principal (Aboriginal Programs) for School District (Sooke) she has developed a positive working relationship with and respect for the Scia'new, T'Sou-ke and Pacheedaht Nations, as well as numerous Aboriginal organizations involved in education. Over the past eight years, she has worked in collaboration with Aboriginal communities to promote literacy, meaningful and trusting community connection, and raise the profile of the Aboriginal Education Enhancement Agreement goals.

Coming Home to Water

By Nina Munteanu (Toronto, Ontario)

I was born in a small town in the Eastern Townships of Quebec, a gently rolling and verdant farming community, where water—l'eau—bubbles and gurgles in at least two languages.

I spent a lot of my childhood days close to the ground, observing, poking, catching, prodding, destroying and creating. Perhaps it was this early induction to the sensual organic fragrances of soil, rotting leaves and moss that set my path in later life as a limnologist, environmental consultant and writer of eco-fiction.

My mother kept a garden in our back yard that she watered mostly with rain she collected in a large barrel out back. I remember rows of bright dahlias with their button-faces and elegant gladiolas of all colours, tall like sentinels. In the winter, my mother would flood the garden to create an ice rink for the neighbourhood to use for hockey. Somehow, I always ended up being the goalie, dodging my brother's swift pucks to the net.

Our dad frequently took us to the local spring just outside town. We walked a few miles up Mountain Road to an unassuming seepage from a rock outcrop with a pipe attached to it by the local farmer. I remember that the water was very cold. Even the air around the spring was cooler than the surrounding air. I remember that the spring water tasted fresh and that the ice it formed popped and fizzed more than tap water ice.

I followed my older brother and sister to the nearby forest and local stream. We stirred soil, flower petals and other interesting things with water to fuel "magic potions" that we inflicted on some poor insect. Yes, I was a bit destructive as a

child—and I took a lot for granted. Like water. There was so much of it, after all. It was clean and easily accessed, fresh from the tap. We fished in the Yamaska River. We often went to Roxton Pond to picnic and swim. I was blissfully unaware of the scarcity of water in other parts of the world; that in many places women my mother's age and girls my age walked for hours to some dubious watering hole to gather water to cook and bathe with; or that within a short few decades some states in North America would make the collection of rainwater illegal or shut off the water to homes of poor citizens unable to pay their tax.

In the 1980s, I journeyed with my close friend Margaret to Tanzania, Kenya and Rwanda. We travelled with a small eco-tour company, camping and riding off-road. There, I met water scarcity head on. We had to conserve for drinking and bathing; most of us on the tour got sick from the local water. When I returned to Canada, I couldn't enter a mall or park—with its profligate displays and water excesses—without feeling shell-shocked. Africa had changed me. It had shifted my worldview and perspective forever. What I'd known intellectually, I now felt viscerally.

I was already pursuing a profession in limnology and began to write eco-fiction. Most of my stories explored dystopias of collapsed ecosystems based on humanity's lack of vision and respect. I became cynical.

When I gave birth to my son, Kevin, I felt a miracle pass through me. Kevin became my doorway back to wonder. His curiosity was boundless and lured me into a special world of transformation.

I took time off work to spend with Kevin when he was young. We went on great trips, from the local mall, where we had a hot chocolate and played with Lego, to the local beach on the Fraser River, where we explored the rocks. When he was no more

than three, I took him on endless adventures in the city and its surroundings. We didn't have to go far. The mud puddles of a new subdivision after a rain were enough to keep our attention for dozens of minutes. We became connoisseurs of mud. The best kind was "chocolate mud," with a consistency and viscosity that created the best crater when a rock was thrown into it.

Kevin and I often explored the little woodland near our house. We made "magic potions" out of nightshade flowers, fir needles, loam and moss; we fuelled our concoctions with the elixir of water from a stagnant pool. This time the little insects weren't molested.

In 2007, I created my first blog, The Alien Next Door. It featured my observations and thoughts as a writer and aquatic ecologist. My profile recounted my favourite things; one of them was walking in the rain, hearing its rhythms and the smell of the Earth after a rainstorm. I was connecting with the liberating and energizing nature of rain and water vapour.

In truth, I was reconnecting with my own nature. And inhaling the scent of a shifting breeze. I would eventually transcend my traditional science; I would leave my hometown and my family to travel alone, meet archetypes who would lead me through swamp, quagmire and salty ocean, as well as crystal lake and rushing brook.

More and more, I've become fascinated by the interrelatedness of things in space–time, particularly in ways that can't be explained. Coincidence, precognition, déjà vu—these all appear to play a shadow-dance with each other. Quantum mechanics shows us that not only is "solid" matter made up mostly of energy and "empty" space, but also what makes a solid a chair (versus you sitting on it) is the vibration of its energy. Quantum science has demonstrated that light and matter are made of both particles and waves that can exist simultaneously. Schrodinger's cat is mystical and quantum entangled. That mystical cat braved the notion that particles can be linked in such a way that changing the quantum state of one instantaneously affects the other, even if they are light years apart. What does it mean when solid flows, ghost-like, through itself under certain conditions? In my trilogy Splintered Universe, one person's past is another's future. And where do they meet? Perhaps in dreams?

As a practicing limnologist, I examined water for its physical and chemical properties. Water was H_2O. I never thought to appreciate its quantum properties.

Water is the bold light of change. Water is the deep purity of soul. Water is who and what we are.

As we enter the seventh golden age, the nirvana of my soul consciousness rejoices with the water of my birth. All that we experienced since childhood has been mingled with the nature of our birthplace. Ultimately, we are connected in family and community through the watershed of our home. I will always feel connected to my birthplace. Its water is my water.

Now, as I roam the world as writer itinerant—travelling and teaching and learning—I find myself grateful for all that I have experienced and learned. Even the "bad" stuff, for even it has gifted me with blessings and opportunities.

Travelling the world has helped me realize that I was blessed with an abundance of water. I lived my entire life in a country of plentiful and healthy water. And for most of that time I didn't even realize it. Canada holds one fifth of the world's fresh water in lakes, rivers, and wetlands, as well as in our underground aquifers and glaciers. Canada's wetlands, which cover more than 1.2 million square kilometres, make Canada the largest wetland area in the world.

Perhaps it is no coincidence that Canada is steward of the world's largest wetlands. Wetlands include marshes, swamps, fens, and bogs, all irreplaceable habitat for a huge diversity of nesting, feeding and staging waterfowl, reptiles, amphibians and mammals—many at risk. Wetlands provide a major filtration system, removing contaminants, improving water quality and renewing water's vitality; wetlands serve as reservoirs, controlling and reducing flooding toward a more balanced hydrological cycle. Wetlands are a source of oxygen and water vapour, serving a vital role in our global atmospheric and climatic cycles. As ecotones—transitional areas—wetlands protect coasts from erosion and provide exceptional opportunity for boundary interaction and the emergence of vitality. Like a good metaphor, wetlands "recognize" and encompass similarities between dissimilarities. Wetlands powerfully connect. Canada's strong multi-cultural policies and its open tolerance in embracing and celebrating diversity make it the "wetland" of the world.

When I turn on the water tap in my house in Canada, it is pure drinking water. I don't need to boil it or filter it or test it for impurities and toxins. I am confident that it will nourish and hydrate me like water should. I can bathe without restriction. I can play with it.

My water hasn't changed; but I have. I do not take it for granted. I know that I am blessed.

I am home and I am so grateful.

Nina Munteanu is an award-winning Canadian ecologist and novelist. In addition to eight published novels, she has authored short stories, articles and non-fiction books, which have been translated into several languages throughout the world. She is currently an editor of European zine Europa SF and Eagle Publishing House and writes for Amazing Stories. Nina teaches writing at George Brown College and the University of Toronto. Her latest book is "Water Is..." a scientific study and personal journey as limnologist, mother, teacher and environmentalist.

Hockey Dad

By Scott Austin (Summerland, BC)

Sam Austin (Captain, Summerland Jets)

It's game two of a three game series. Our team, the Summerland Midget Rep Jets trail 1-0 in games and our boys are down 4-3 with less than a minute left. We pull the goalie for an extra skater, and my son Sam is on the blue line to my right as I sit in the scorekeeper's box at ice level. The dream ending goes like this: the puck comes to Sam, he steps into a shot and drives it into the net for the tying goal. Reality, however, is somewhat different. The puck skips on him and he can't hold the line. Sam skates back for the puck and turns up ice, but I watch the time tick away and a lump forms in my throat.

Eleven years of minor hockey have come down to a few seconds. The horn sounds, the players shake hands and I see the #11 on the back of my son's jersey as he skates off the ice and disappears into the hall.

I knew back when the season started in October that this moment was going to arrive, and now it was here. After passing the scoresheet over to the referee I made my way into the arena lobby. It was packed as usual with parents: those who were celebrating a win and those who weren't. Our group was probably contemplating what a free weekend would look like.

Sam emerged from the dressing room and we walked out into the parking lot and left a lifetime of memories behind us.

I never played minor hockey, but I grew up playing hockey in our driveway, on the road, in friends' driveway, in the school gym. We would play in the dark, in the snow, Saturday night between periods of Hockey Night in Canada and in our dreams. I was a Canadiens fan, then a Canucks fan after 1970. I never pushed Sam to play hockey, but he was keen right from the start. I was secretly excited when I took him to his first practice. The pint-sized hockey team for 5-6 year-olds was appropriately called the Summerland Squirts.

Sam was never a great skater but he was a smart, team-oriented player. From an early age he looked for open teammates and fed them soft passes. He scored the occasional goal, usually off rebounds in front of the net, where he was fearless, taking all kinds of abuse to establish position. Yet during his first years, he was a shy kid who couldn't skate backwards. Ironic that in his final year of Midget Rep he played defence, having never played the position before and was named captain of his team.

Hockey had done so much for Sam and it really defined our father-son relationship. So many of our best times together have revolved around the game. We've travelled to arenas all over southern British Columbia, in snowstorms and in bright sunshine. We've eaten too much Chinese food during team dinners on the road and watched so many hockey games that I long ago lost count.

Through it all, I've treasured every moment. He played, I watched. It was that way for eleven winters.

Yet, truth be known, it almost wasn't that way at all.

Sam was born 11 weeks premature at BC Children's Hospital. He weighed just 2 pounds, 14 ounces and had to be resuscitated at birth as he had no heartbeat. He spent his first two months in an incubator and had numerous medical issues. But he survived. He grew to be a big strapping boy with broad shoulders. Anything he accomplished on the ice was a miracle to me because of the circumstances of his birth. When he scored a goal or threaded a pass I outwardly cheered but inside I said a prayer of gratitude.

Although not all will admit it, every hockey dad has a secret desire for his son to play in the NHL. I had that dream for Sam too, but fortunately for both of us it didn't last too long. I was able to see hockey for what it was doing for my son and how much he loved to be on the ice and be part of a team. When I think back on my time as a hockey dad I won't remember the puck skipping over his stick at the end of his last game. I'll remember tournament victories, kids' smiles bursting out from behind their cages and earnest conversations in the car about where we're going to eat after the game. I'll also remember the goal he scored in his first year of Midget Rep in the first game of our home tournament. We played our rivals from South Okanagan. There were six minutes left in the third period and the score was tied 4-4. Sam blocked a shot at our blue line, grabbed the puck and skated past one defenceman. He then outhustled the second defenceman, moved in on the goalie, deked him backhand-forehand and slid the puck by him for the winning goal.

That was my son. I'm his dad, and that goal was better than Henderson in '72, Lemieux in '87 and Crosby in Olympic overtime.

(Sam and I at a Canucks-Leafs hockey game)

Scott Austin is nursery manager for GardenWorks Penticton, garden writer and host of 'Garden Talk' on Easy Rock radio stations. He has lived and raised his family in Summerland for most of his life. The Austins are avid hockey fans.

My Father-in-Law's
LEGACY

By Deborah Fike (Eugene, Oregon)

(Bill Fike holding his grandchild)

In the Moment — Real Life Stories of Hope and Inspiration

Most people are nervous when they meet their boyfriend's or girlfriend's parents for the first time, but my first meeting had special circumstances. Given his parents' conservative nature, my boyfriend worried they wouldn't like me, a blue-haired, recently divorced video game marketing professional that had already moved in with their son. On the way to the airport, my boyfriend mulled this over in his mind, tapping out an email message on his phone as I drove.

"What are you writing?" I asked as we pulled into a parking space.

"One second," he replied. Then with finality, he tapped a button and closed his phone. "Done. I just sent an email to my parents laying down the law."

'The law,' in this case, was my boyfriend's fervent, but unfortunately misplaced, attempt to keep things civil. He insisted that he was 'in love' and if they didn't 'accept that' and 'treat me well,' then he wouldn't speak to them ever again.

Needless to say, I had butterflies in my stomach when I met his folks on the other side of that plane ride. My boyfriend's mother kept her polite distance in the kind of way you expect a customer service representative to deal with an irate customer.

My boyfriend's father Bill, however, was all charm and grace. He gave me a smile and a hug, blue hair and all. His booming laugh put me at ease, and I remember feeling relieved to see well-used crow's feet near his eyes. My boyfriend's mom would warm up to me later in the weekend, but I was already on board with Dad. His son's love, apparently, was enough for him from the beginning.

From that moment at the airport onward, from dating my boyfriend, to becoming engaged, married, and then having children, Bill defined our relationship with warmth and kindness. We did not see eye-to-eye on many things – certainly not politics or religion – but it didn't matter to him. You could have serious discussions with Bill and keep it to the issues without it ever feeling like a personal attack. I learned from his perspective, and he told me he learned from mine. Debates with him felt like an exchange of ideas, not a line drawn in the sand.

I also discovered where my husband inherited his playfulness. Bill had a pool table in the upstairs rec room. He loved playing golf with his sons whenever he could get them together. After I had children, he went from bouncing babies on his knee to singing silly songs from his own youth to making glittery jewelry boxes with my preschooler. He would not hesitate to play dolls if asked by his grandchild. When we went with him to Disneyland for the first time, I don't know who enjoyed it more: the children or him. He rode everything from the kiddie rides to the roller coasters, reveling in the spectacle of it all.

Bill's joyous outlook at the world defined him, which is why we all knew something was terribly wrong last summer when he began to falter. He felt tired all of the time and couldn't maintain his interest in things he loved. He visited us once across the country and spent most of the time in his room, sleeping or resting. I remember he came down one evening and acted like his old self: getting involved in a conversation with my husband, mother-in-law and myself on the latest political antics and family goings-on. But other than that, he was weak, not himself. My daughter didn't get her normal art time with him, so instead she sat silently in his lap, cuddling with him as he stared into the distance.

The stage 4 pancreatic cancer diagnosis later in the month shouldn't have been a shock, but it was. Everyone hoped for a brighter prognosis at least, but Bill was given weeks at best. In fact, he would pass away within days.

In those final days, I took care of the children while my husband stayed by my-father-in-law's side along with the rest of his family. He rapidly lost weight and was in tremendous pain. He lived in a world of foggy confusion, but he sometimes had moments of crystal clarity when he knew everything that was going on around him.

If ever there was a time when you would forgive someone for withdrawing into themselves, it would be this: reduced to a hospital bed fighting a battle for your life that you will lose, sooner rather than later. Bill, though, continued to commit his life to loving his family. He underwent several treatments hoping to extend his life by a little, mostly for his wife. On the last such surgery, he pulled my husband aside and asked him to look after his mother after he was gone. He made sure to say good-bye to everyone he could when he had the chance.

In the face of death, Bill chose love yet again.

(Continued on the next page)

Deborah Fike is the the founder of Avalon Labs, which provides marketing consultations and writing services for start-ups and online businesses. She carves out a significant portion of her time to raising her two young daughters.

After he passed away, the outpouring of love and support came from everywhere. Not only family and close friends, but co-workers from long ago, friends from childhood, and even friends of friends came by to give their respects to Bill. His memorial was swathed in a rainbow of flowers sent from far off places from people he had not seen in years. His legacy of love followed him literally to his grave.

The world certainly is a lesser place without Bill. I miss our chats where I learned about my husband's history. I mourn that my daughters lost such a wonderful grandfather. My heart aches for my husband, who wishes for just one more round of golf.

But to dwell solely on what we lost truly misses Bill's legacy, a legacy he left through everyone who knew him. I see Bill out of the corner of my eye as my daughter bends over the art table, determined to finish coloring her masterpiece. I can hear him when my brother-in-law laughs at a joke in the other room. And certainly, I can feel Bill's presence when my husband plays with my girls, his childlike joy an exact copy of his father's.

Bill is still here with us because he left the best thing behind: his love.

(Bill Fike coloring with his granddaughter)

In the Moment — Real Life Stories of Hope and Inspiration

Two Jack Lake

(Banff National Park; Photo Credit: Christopher Martin)

©CHC

Frank Selke, Manager, Montreal Canadiens

Waiting was painful. Not knowing what would happen was even worse. I wasn't good at either—waiting or wondering.

My turn was coming up. I'd be meeting "the man"—Mr. Frank Selke, General Manager of the illustrious Montreal Canadiens—the most powerful person in hockey. I was one of several goalies invited to the September, 1955 Montreal training camp but I wasn't sure what my chances were. I could be offered a professional contract or sent home packing. In my mind, I was prepared for anything.

The office door opened and out walked Henri Richard, the younger brother of hockey great Maurice (the Rocket) Richard. He smiled when he saw me sitting in the reception area but left without saying a word. Henri was a sure bet to sign with the club.

MEETING 'THE MAN'

By Ivan McLelland (Penticton, BC)

My dream to be a goalie in the National Hockey League (NHL) started when I was fourteen years old. I remember huddling around a radio with teammates on a Saturday night listening to the Boston Bruins play the Toronto Maple Leafs. It was Turk Broda (Maple Leaf clutch goaltender) versus Frank Brimsek (Boston legend "Mr. Zero"). I just knew I was going to be like one of them, someday.

I learned to face shooters of all varieties and earned a reputation as a tough kid with an amazing glove hand. 1943 was the first year I played goalie in the juvenile hockey league in South Porcupine, Ontario. A year later, I helped my team win it all—the Ontario Juvenile Hockey championship.

My big break came years later in 1951 when I was invited to tryout with the Vancouver Canucks, the farm team for the New York Rangers. I had never been outside my home Province of Ontario so this was a big adventure. I was both nervous and excited about travelling by train across the country to Vancouver.

I performed well in training camp but not well enough to secure the number one goalie position. Instead, the Canucks general manager offered me the goaltending job with the Penticton Vees, a senior men's hockey team in the Okanagan Valley. I would also be the back-up goalie for the Vancouver Canucks, if and when required. I decided to accept the offer.

It turned out to be the best thing that could have happened. Penticton became my new home—not only did I play on a championship team, I also met my future wife there.

1954 was a miraculous year. Our team, the Penticton Vees, was led by the three Warwick brothers including Captain and Coach Grant Warwick, the 1942 rookie-of-the-year with the New York Rangers. We

were the Western Canadian Champions for the second year in a row. Next up was the Allan Cup, the "holy grail" of amateur hockey in Canada. We failed in our bid to win-it-all the previous year. This time we were up against the Eastern Canadian Champions, the Sudbury Wolves.

We had a disastrous start. We were down three games to one in the best-of-seven series. After the third loss, I was devastated as we had dug ourselves a deep hole. Somehow we had to turn it around or our time as a contending team would pass. Some of my teammates spoke out about our predicament in the dressing room prior to the next game. We knew we had to start fresh, to begin again. We must have taken it to heart because we managed to win big—not just the next game—but for the next three straight games! It was a remarkable comeback.

Now we were faced with the heady task and responsibility of representing Canada on the world stage. In March, 1955, the hockey world was buzzing about the team representing Canada. Penticton, a rural community (population 11,000) was competing against the world's best in Europe. We were a town better known for growing peaches than hockey. Vedette, Valiant and Veteran were not names of famous hockey players but three varieties of local peaches. Hence, the name "Vees". We were the classic underdogs. Yet during the tournament in Dusseldorf, Germany, we silenced our critics by amassing a perfect 8-0 record. We scored 66 goals and only allowed in six. I recorded 4 shut-outs.

The gold medal game against the defending champion USSR was the ultimate contest for hockey supremacy. It was also a clash of ideologies, pitting the free world against the socialists and everything the Iron Curtain represented.

The game opened with the Russians

skating strongly, carrying much of the play. A rash of penalties against Canada led to numerous scoring chances for the Russians. However, we managed to hold them off and gradually put together a solid defensive and offensive game. The final score was 5-0, a decisive win for Canada. The pride of the nation was restored.

It was a dream come true.

But would that dream continue? I was now twenty-six years old. Any decision I made about a hockey career would need to consider my family—my wife Faye and two children. Yet I wanted a professional contract. Or, at least to be offered one. I certainly didn't want to be cut from the squad.

After twelve years of playing organized hockey, my body bore the scars. Pucks travelling 90 mph broke face bones and smashed teeth. Goalies in those days didn't wear hockey masks and helmets. Sometimes I played injured, once with a broken wrist that had to be frozen to manage the pain. I had over 100 stitches in my upper body.

I was ushered into Mr. Selke's private office. Mr. Selke sat behind a rather large desk talking on the telephone. I was taken aback when I first saw him. I had expected someone more imposing, more distinguished looking. He was small and wore glasses, his greying hair in a brush cut.

I sat down in the plush leather chair facing his desk and waited. When he hung up the phone, he barely acknowledged me. There was no small talk to make me feel at ease or welcome. He just looked directly at me, and in a business-like manner, laid it on the line.   "You have great potential," he said. "We've decided to offer you a contract with the Montreal Canadiens. I'll be perfectly honest with you though. You won't be playing with the Canadiens." He then went on to say that I

(Ivan McLelland, 1955 World Hockey Tournament)

would be assigned to their American league affiliate in Rochester, New York.

"We think you need further professional experience, perhaps two years," he said. "You may never play with our team. You could very well be traded to another NHL club. If you have a good year or two, you could wind up in the NHL. You have the potential." As he spoke he removed papers from a file along with what appeared to be a cheque.

"We are prepared to pay you the sum of $3,500 to become a professional player," he added. "With that you become the property of the Montreal Canadiens. We reserve the right to either sell or trade you to another organization. The contract states you will be paid $4,000 a year to play in the American Hockey League and $7,500 if you play in the NHL."

I listened intently. Everything seemed to be happening so fast. I didn't know whether to be excited or worried. At least I wasn't being cut.

"Well Ivan," he said, "do you have any questions?"

"Yes sir." I replied. "Mr. Selke, what would happen if I was called up from Rochester to play in Montreal? Or, say you decide to send me to Seattle in the Western league?"

"Well, son, you'd be required to report and play there for as long as you are needed," he said. "That's what we are paying you to do."

"And my family? I have a young family. What if I bring them to Rochester?"

"Well, we always try and accommodate families, but quite frankly it's not always possible."

"Sorry to ask all these questions Mr. Selke," I said not wanting to sound ungrateful for his contract offer. "If I was called up to Montreal for a month, then my family would be alone in Rochester?"

"Entirely possible." He paused and

added, "Ivan, if you intend to become a professional goalie you must understand it can be difficult on families."

"Please understand this. We have in excess of seventy players in our system," he said. "If I had to be concerned with every player's family and what arrangements they made, I could not possibly run our business. Could I?"

"I suppose not," I said. "Mr. Selke, could I have some time to think this over?"

"I thought you came to camp ready to become a Montreal Canadien?"

"Well sir, I came to camp to have a look-see. I wanted to know how I'd stack up against professional players."

The room became quiet for a few moments.

"Well, son, you know the details. I will make you an appointment for tomorrow morning, at which time we will determine whether or not you intend to sign this contract."

There was no further discussion as Mr. Selke turned his attention to another file on his desk.

That night, I spoke with my wife about the meeting and what life would be like as a minor league professional hockey player. The more we talked about it, the more certain I became. It wasn't the life for me or my family. Players were viewed as "possessions" to be moved around at the will of their owners, much like ranchers moving cattle from field to field. With only six teams in the league, the team owners ran the show.

The next morning I met with Mr. Selke to let him know my decision. It may not have been the answer he wanted or expected but he did extend an invitation to attend training camp the following season. And then the meeting was over. We did not even shake hands. We were done.

I had sealed my fate. The dream I had nurtured since childhood was ending.

The long flight home that day would provide plenty of time for reflection and soul-searching. Yet I had no regrets about my decision. In fact, I felt a deep sense of relief.

I didn't want the nomadic life of a professional hockey goalie. I would honour my agreement to play one more year for the Penticton Vees, but while doing that, I would begin my search for a new life away from the hockey world.

When I arrived at my destination that evening and walked into the Penticton airport terminal, I knew I had made the right decision. There, waiting to welcome me with open arms was Faye, the love of my life, and our two wonderful children, David and Bonnie.

It was so good to be home again. I had been gone long enough.

(Goalie Ivan McLelland competing in the 1955 World Hockey Tournament)

(Ivan poses in front of Penticton's Memorial Arena, 2016)

During the Vees run-up to the 1954 National Championship which qualified them to be selected to the Worlds in 1955, **Ivan McLelland** played every minute of the 102 hockey games. (A remarkable achievement considering that Ivan did not even wear a face guard!) At the World Tournament he played all eight games registering an amazing GAA (Goals Against Average) of .075 and 4 shutouts. To this day, that record has not been equalled or surpassed.

Ivan was inducted into the BC Hockey Hall of Fame (1994), BC Sports Hall of Fame (2005) and the Timmins Sports Heritage Hall of Fame (2014). In 2012 Ivan documented his hockey journey in a wonderful memoir titled, "Gold Mine to Gold Medal and Beyond" (www.goldminetogoldmedal.com).

Ivan's career after hockey was equally successful and rewarding. Ivan started out as a salesman for the Nielson Chocolate Company and quickly advanced through the company ranks to become the Regional Manager for British Columbia. At the same time, Ivan dedicated his life to helping others. He has been and continues to be an enthusiastic ambassador for hockey and a steadfast fundraiser for various charities including: the Good Samaritan Village by the Station and the Alzheimer's Society.

MOMENT OF JOY

(Hanna, Alberta; Photo Credit: Cole Hofstra)

(BC Regiment "The Dukes", Photo Credit: Claude P. Dettloff, Province Newspaper, 1940)

Wait For Me, Daddy

By Canon W.D. (Whitey) Bernard (Tofino, BC)

"People around the world know the photo, but most don't know that it was taken in New Westminster, BC, Canada. On October 1, 1940, newspaper photographer Claude P. Dettloff was photographing The British Columbian Regiment march down 8th Street enroute to battle overseas. In a random moment, Dettloff snapped a photo of a young, white-haired boy, escape his mother's grasp and run towards his father marching off to war. That photo titled 'Wait for Me Daddy' became an enduring symbol of Canada's WWII effort."

- City of New Westminster website (WaitForMeDaddy.com)

I was there. Yet, I don't remember that day, let alone that moment. But, I was only five years old at the time. That's me in the photograph: the young, white-haired boy.

Everyone calls me 'Whitey'. My real name is Warren Bernard, the name given to me by my parents, Bernice and Jack Bernard.

What I do remember is the next day. The Province newspaper published a full page picture of me in action as I called out "Wait for me, Daddy". My family and friends all talked about it. That's what I remember.

The 'Wait For Me, Daddy' image was reprinted around the world during the war, beginning with Life magazine. It was featured on recruiting and fund-raising posters across Canada and posted in schools, legion halls and government offices. When I was 8 years old, I was 'drafted' to assist in the Victory Bond Drive. The organizers asked Mom for permission to include me in some of the campaigns to raise money. The campaigns were six weeks long, so I had to be excused from school, which I didn't mind at all. I'd wear my navy blazer, white shirt and short pants and join the entertainers (singers and dancers). We'd put on shows at various war production facilities and ship-yards.

"When you look at the picture," I would say to the crowd as I pointed to the poster, "think of Canada's little boys and girls who want their daddies home. That's why we ask you to buy a bond today." My name was never advertised. The organizers referred to me as the 'boy in service'.

Dad enlisted as a private with the BC Regiment, Duke of Connaught's Own Rifles, also known as the "Dukes". Mom wanted him to wait to be called up with his regular regiment, the BCDs (the B.C. Dragoons) where he was the acting troop sergeant major. But as the unit was not activated until much later, my dad dropped his rank to join the "Dukes" and we moved from Summerland in the Okanagan Valley to Vancouver in 1940. A year later Dad was promoted to sergeant.

After he joined the army, Mom and I were alone in the big city, without family and friends. To make ends meet, my mother worked long hours all week at a manufacturing plant, including Saturday mornings. So I learned to fend for myself at a young age. I left for school on my own and came home to an empty house.

My school principal found out that my mother wasn't around a lot and reported us to the Social Services department. One day, a welfare lady appeared at our home; she was well-dressed wearing a full-length fur coat.

"Mrs. Bernard," she said calmly. "There are some things you need to change. Your son needs better care. You should be here when he comes home from school. He would also benefit from eating wholesome foods such as oranges."

Mom was furious when she heard that. "How dare you come in here and tell me what to do. I can't afford oranges on a sergeant's pay!"

"Well, if you can't do these things," she said, "then maybe it would be better for your son to live with someone else."

"Okay, that's it. Get out of here!" Mom shouted and the conversation ended.

Not long after, we moved to another area

(The day my dad came home; Photo Credit: Claude P. Dettloff, 1945)

In the Moment — Real Life Stories of Hope and Inspiration

of town and I went to a different school. It was like we were on the run.

I remember a time I saw Mom crying as she read the 'missing in action' and 'killed in action' lists in the newspaper. Besides my dad, we had uncles, cousins and neighbours on active service in Burma, Sicily, England and Europe. Cousin Hector lost a leg and Johnny (from down the street) fell down a well in Italy. When I visited my friend Gary, he told me his father was 'missing in action' and did not come home.

In 1943 Dad returned on short-term leave at Christmastime. I was in grade three. At the time my mom and I lived in a store-front at 8th and Burrard in Vancouver. Even though my dad came to visit, he didn't stay with us, which confused me. My dad and I spent a fun-packed day together. I saw Santa Claus at Spencer's Department Store, rode the Christmas train, did the 'fish pond' and visited with Grandpa. We even had lunch in a restaurant!

After we arrived home Mom and Dad went into the kitchen to talk and I curled up on the couch as the kids' radio show was on. I listened for a while but my attention soon turned to the raised voices in the kitchen. Mom and Dad were yelling, swearing and threatening each other. Then I heard a loud crash. Dad had flipped the table over, breaking the teapot and smashing the Christmas cake on the floor. The room became very quiet after that, except for Mom's sobbing. It was upsetting. I felt so scared and helpless.

When Dad came to say goodbye, he had a pained expression on his face. He opened his mouth to say something but no words came out. As he turned to leave, he managed a smile and said, "I am sorry, Buck. You will have to look out for yourself 'til I come back." He always called me 'Buck'.

Three weeks later he was back in England with the 6th Canadian Armoured Regiment (1st Hussars) CAC of the 2nd Canadian Armoured Brigade. The unit was in the thick of the D-Day campaign through June, 1944 and Dad joined the regiment in Normandy on July 4 as a reinforcement in "C" Squadron. They were involved in the major campaigns through France, participated in the liberation of the Netherlands and carried on into Germany in 1945.

The happiest day in my then 10-year-old life was when Dad returned home at war's end, safe at last. He had survived the war. However, his marriage did not and Mom and Dad went their separate ways. The 'Wait For Me, Daddy' photo was the last record of us together as a family.

Seventy four years later, on October 4, 2014, I was in the limelight again.

Mayor Wayne Wright and Council of New Westminster had a bold vision to create a war memorial sculpture, based on 'Wait for me, Daddy'. To this end, the city council commissioned internationally acclaimed sculptors Veronica and Edwin Dam De Nogales. Councillor Lorrie Williams served as the Task Force Chair for the project. At the same time, the Federal government and The Royal Canadian Mint dedicated three coins to the famous scene: a general circulation $2 coin, and commemorative issues in $3 and $10 denominations. Canada Post also issued a general circulation stamp depicting the 'Wait For Me, Daddy' image.

The celebratory event became a triple unveiling ceremony and was held at Hyack Square, the exact location where the famous war-time photo was taken. It was a magnificent display of acknowledgement and remembrance. I was deeply touched by what transpired that historic day.

Sometimes I wonder what my parents, who died many years earlier, would think of all the attention. No doubt, my mother would have been pleased. She liked how the photo spoke to families about the anxiety, worry, separation and loss they faced during that difficult time. My father's response would have been more subdued. He was mostly silent about his war experience after he returned in 1945. The war took so much out of him and he didn't want to revisit the dark memories. Yet, at the same time, he'd want to honour his comrades-in-arms who fought so bravely. My dad would probably have a gentle smile and a quiet 'thank you' to all those who were there with him, in person and in spirit.

As for me, well, I am just grateful. I'm grateful to everyone for keeping the memory alive. In many ways 'Wait For Me, Daddy' is as relevant today as it was 75 years ago. The image is a heartfelt reminder of the human cost of war on families and loved ones, at home and abroad.

A lesson I learned far too early in life when I was just a young, white-haired boy.

In the Moment — Real Life Stories of Hope and Inspiration

Whitey Bernard has shown an outstanding dedication and commitment to public service throughout his life. He has served in many roles, including: a volunteer fireman and deputy fire chief, a little league coach, President and life member of the Royal Canadian Legion (Branch 65), people's warden at St. Columbia Anglican Church, Tofino mayor and councillor, an advisor to Ducks Unlimited and director/secretary-treasurer of the Tofino Salmon Enhancement Society. Whitely is also a Lay Canon in the Anglican Church of Canada (Diocese of BC).

Whitey lives in the "most beautiful part of BC"— Tofino on the west coast of Vancouver Island. Whitely and his wife Ruby recently celebrated their 50th wedding anniversary. Together they have three children and three grandchildren. He also has a daughter and three more grandchildren from a previous marriage.

For more information about the 'Wait For Me Daddy' history and monument in New Westminster BC, check out the website: waitformedaddy.com

(On the left: Wait For Me, Daddy statue)

Compiled by Gary Doi

Whitey Bernard & grandchildren pose in front of statue (Photo credit: City of New Westminster)

In the Moment — Real Life Stories of Hope and Inspiration

Thanks to
the following
COMMUNITY
PARTNERS

for their
generous
support!

"Back to the Mountain"
— Roy Henry Vickers

Compiled by Gary Doi

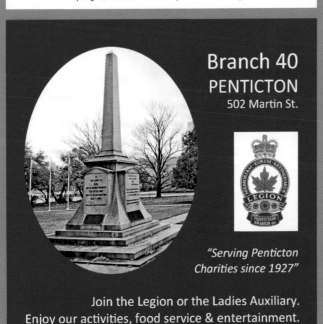

Compiled by Gary Doi

NEW WESTMINSTER

It's Monumental

After reading Whitey Bernard's story, you'll want to visit Hyack Square, the exact location where the "Wait For Me, Daddy" photo was taken. The City of New Westminster commissioned the war memorial to honour the famous photo which reminds us all of the human cost of war, at home and abroad.

Compiled by Gary Doi

TOFINO, BC
A Great Place to Work and Play

GEAR FOR OUT HERE

Storm Light
OUTFITTERS

Method Marine Supply
380 Main Street, Tofino B.C.
250-725-3251

Tofino Fishing and Trading
Campbell & 4th Street, Tofino B.C.
250-725-2622

Ocean West Marina & Property
389 Main Street, Tofino B.C.
250-725-3256

Storm Light Outfitters
389 Main Street, Tofino B.C.
250-725-3342

"Owned and operated by Whitey, Ruby, Steve, Cathy & Karyn Bernard"

Compiled by Gary Doi